Praise for *Shake Yourself Free*

"Melanie Smithson's writing speaks directly to the heart with clarity, compassion, and a playfulness that makes even the deepest work feel accessible. Her latest book offers practices that are transformative, opening space for joy and connection. In my experience, as a single mom and former CEO, these tools offer so much help in the emotional demands of life; they are invaluable in navigating the stress, complexity, and interpersonal challenges of motherhood and leadership. Melanie's work is a gift—practical, profound, and full of possibility. If you want to feel better, get this book and play with the movement."

Tiffany Grunert, Leadership Consultant

"Shake Yourself Free is a gift for anyone ready to release the weight of life's stressors and reclaim their freedom—both emotional and physical. Melanie Smithson masterfully guides readers to let the body take center stage, revealing what we've been holding on to that no longer serves us. Through her simple yet profound body-centered techniques, she offers a clear, compassionate path to letting go. You'll be deeply grateful to carry these tools with you, whether navigating everyday life or moving through life's most stressful moments."

Dianne Maroney, RN, MSN, Author, Founder and Executive Director of The Imagine Project, Inc.

"*Shake Yourself Free* is a valuable resource for those looking to develop effective movement practices that support freedom and aliveness. The content is accessible, with suggestions that are straightforward and easy to integrate. Whether the goal is enhanced productivity or personal development, the book supplies practical, actionable methods. Readers could pick it up and begin anywhere or read cover to cover. I would recommend this book to any of my coaching clients and to other coaching professionals seeking tactical approaches to support connection to the body. The world needs what Melanie has to say. She is on to something wonderful."

Deanell Sandoval, Leadership, Life and Wellness Coach

"*Shake Yourself Free* is a must-have inspiration and resource for those who see growth, healing and aliveness as a way of life. Therapists, coaches, and leaders can use and enjoy it for themselves and with their clients, both during sessions and as a resource recommendation. Letting go works. Somatic therapy works. Melanie craftily combines both in this book, setting it apart as a 'one of a kind.' She presents the 81 practices in an easy, doable form. They are workable, playful and enjoyable. I recommend this book wholeheartedly."

Ginny Swem, NLC, CH, Psychotherapist

"Both a thought-provoking and thought-dissolving book, *Shake Yourself Free*, is full of profound practices to support you in your quest to freedom. Rather than working hard to figure out why you suffer, Smithson offers easy movement practices to transform and dissolve what holds you back. This comprehensive guide should be required reading for any practicing therapist."

Jackie Chivers, Author, Former Director and Award-winner of Athena Counselling Services Ltd

"Smithson offers a fun process to connect with your internal wisdom, strength and authenticity. Drawing on her vast knowledge of the psyche and the body's role in healing, she has created a comprehensive guide for moving through what holds you back so you can move ahead."

Anne Salisbury, PhD, MBA, Intuitive Psychotherapist, Hypnotherapist, Business Consultant and Award-winning Author

Shake Yourself Free

81 SOMATIC PRACTICES TO LET GO OF LIMITATION

MELANIE SMITHSON

Shake Yourself Free: 81 Somatic Practices to Let Go of Limitation by **Melanie Smithson**

Printed in the United States of America by **Komodia Press**

First Edition
ISBN: 978-8-9998660-5-9

Book Cover Design and Interior Formatting by 100Covers

TABLE OF CONTENTS

To my dance and movement teachers, and all dedicated to imparting the wisdom and transformation that is possible through the body and movement.

And especially to Chloe Goodwin, the space and community you have created, coupled with the wisdom that is you, allowed the material to come to life in me.

INTRODUCTION

Many years ago, I had a conversation with a woman about letting go. I so clearly remember her voice saying, "I would if I could." This has been expressed to me so many times throughout the years in my work as a therapist, but her voice was the one that stayed with me. As a child you knew how to let go. You moved from one emotion to the next in a matter of minutes. But your adult mind complicates things. It has lots of reasons for holding on and justifications for not letting go. This holding on gets in the way of freedom. The body, on the other hand, is more direct and accurate in its communications, but most of us have never learned how to closely listen to our body.

Throughout our lives, we are asked to let go of a million little things, some very big things, and then, eventually, life itself. With every breath, we take in and we let out. When we don't let go, we are holding on and accumulating disturbances in our bodies, psyches and souls. We become *hoarders of upset*. Then we justify, defend and explain the upset to ourselves and anyone who will listen. Over and over, we repeat the story to drive home why we can't or won't let go. We become over-identified with our experiences and then feel defined by them. We justify future action based on our hoarding of upset. And we spiral deeper into disturbance and unhappiness.

Letting go is an innate skill, a natural ability that many have lost touch with. The price we pay for this is suffering, whether it comes in the form of depression, anxiety, physical illness, unhealthy relationships or long-held resentments.

Releasing our held beliefs and emotions supports release in our bodies. And our bodies can also be engaged to help us release our emotions and beliefs. The practice of letting go is a powerful antidote to the vast majority of our problems. **When we let go, we literally lighten up and free ourselves from what we have been holding in our bodies!**

My first career was as an accountant in New York City. My dad was an accountant; I loved numbers; it all made sense. I worked hard to become a Certified Public Accountant and was on track to become a partner in a small firm. But I had a problem. The dance classes I wanted to be in took place during my workday. And the mantra in my head, "I don't want to be here, I want to be dancing," would not shut up. Eventually, the voice in my head won. I quit my job, started managing the dance studio for $50/week, plus all the dance classes I could take. I was in heaven.

An unsustainable heaven, but my life was now on a new path. Fast forward seven years and I was well on my own self-discovery journey; recently married in New Mexico, I found myself in a workshop led by two amazing women. Over the course of three days, I witnessed one woman after another let go of long-held beliefs and traumatic experiences. I saw tears turn to laughter and darkness transition to light. I wouldn't have been able to identify it at the time, but now I can say the facilitators were well-versed in somatic (relating to the body) practices, worked with spirit and intuition, and through compassion and presence created a space where transformation happened.

The shifts these women were able to activate in others amazed me, lit me up and started my wondering how I could contribute to the alleviation of suffering in the world. A few years later, in a movement-based workshop, my love of movement emerged as the way I wanted to support and work with others. Throughout my experiences in those workshops and in attending Naropa University for my master's in dance/movement therapy, I felt the presence of divine guidance, as if the path had already been laid out and I just needed to follow it.

Thirty years later, I am still following, still learning, still practicing. In my sessions with clients, we explore together. We step into a space (even when meeting online) where there is an "invitation to wonder." Far from traditional psychotherapy models, where mentally figuring out is the norm, we check in with physical sensation and allow what's below the surface to reveal itself. This willingness to explore is something my body knows from conscious movement, a practice in which, as one of my teachers is known to say, *we disappear ourselves.* Rather than directing how my body moves, I wait and listen to my body and allow it to inform me on what it wants and needs to move.

A basic premise in the field of dance/movement therapy is that movement has a natural cycle with a beginning, middle and end. Emotions are energy and also have a natural movement sequence. The interruption of this sequence for any reason has consequences for the body and life itself. In dance/movement therapy, we uncover where an emotion has been held in the body and allow and explore what may not have been given expression in the past. The energy may be stuck in the heart or the hip or the throat. Giving that stuck energy some compassionate attention allows it to reveal itself. We wonder how it might want to shift and release through movement. It could be a shake or tremble, a scream, shove, kick or laugh. Releasing the emotion that's been held frees the body and mind from stuck psychological and physical patterns. It's been said, "*Where the mind goes, the body will follow.*" I would argue that the opposite is also true: **"Where the body goes, the mind will follow."**

I feel that the angels (and other wise beings) gave me the material for this book. For several months, every time I danced, different ways to let go were clearly shown to me. I felt them in my body, each one creating a shift in my movement, allowing the release of a thought or feeling and opening new possibilities. Some were familiar from my years of both dance and clinical practice, some were new to me. Every Sunday, in 5Rhythms® class in Santa Fe, information poured in as I moved my body. My dance became a dance with myself, with others and with this book. It was a fascinating process to experience and simultaneously observe. I would dance and feel a new way to let go, or hear something about thinking, or recognize a habit and its impact, and after every two or three such experiences, I would run to my notebook and write for fear of losing what I'd been given, then step back into the dance. And more would come. And I'd write more notes.

Our job is to move ourselves out of the way so the universe can support us in recognizing how much we already have, and in having more of what is in our highest good. I believe the universe wants more for us than we could ever imagine. Letting go allows us to move out of our own way, so we can hear what's beyond the ongoing chatter of our personal mind.

Though the practices in this book came to me through movement, one does not need to be a dancer to tap into the wisdom of the body. The incredible resource of the body is always with us. Its inner wisdom is there for the asking. When able to find fluidity in the joints, flexibility in the world comes with more ease. By softening the relationship with the organs, emotions can be gentler. And in connecting to the spine, taking a stance may become possible.

I describe letting go as a state of being. It is not merely the ceasing of reaction and resistance. To let something go means you have moved all the way through the experience and the related feelings. You feel complete with it. It's not pretending something doesn't bother you. It's learning to come to a place of peace where you no longer feel any attachment or aversion to the person or situation that you were holding on to with anger, grief, loyalty or simply out of habit.

Our natural state, the one we see in infants, is full of curiosity, wonder and exploration. But as we grow older, we develop a tendency to go through the world with opinions, often accompanied by resistance or judgment that keeps us in a contracted and uncomfortable state, physically and emotionally. Letting go is how we interrupt these tendencies.

But letting go doesn't happen as spontaneously as we might like. And telling yourself to let go often doesn't work. Sometimes we know we should let go but don't know how, sometimes we think we shouldn't let go and sometimes we don't even realize letting go is an option. What we do instead is hold on and get in the way of the natural flow of energy. There are many ways we do this, including resisting our current experience, justifying and defending our upset and trying to understand why things are the way they are. If what we really want is freedom, we may need to let go of mentally figuring things out and leave the mind without an answer (poor thing).

Holding on is a physical reflex (another argument for letting go through movement). As infants, grasping happens. As we age, holding on often comes intentionally from a desire to be in control, wanting things the way we want them. This both expresses and reinforces distrust in the universe and in our ability to navigate our lives. **Ironically, our fervent desire to be in control keeps us feeling out of control**, at the mercy of anything that does not line up with our beliefs or desires. We hold on to the ways we feel we've been wronged by others, we hold on to upset about the way the dog behaved, we hold on to grief and so much more. When we don't let go, we are physically contracting and tightening. It takes effort to hold on. When I don't let go, I feel pissy, on edge and annoyed by much more than the initial upset. I don't like that feeling. So, I choose to let go in favor of peace, joy, connection and well-being.

You might already know it would benefit you to let go. Many books about letting go offer wonderful exercises—including breath, mindfulness, journaling and verbal practices. But I have found none that use movement to support release. It's time for the body to take center stage.

The body is full of wisdom, often ignored or unacknowledged. When we neglect the body's role in letting go, we risk limiting ourselves to a surface-level release, which can result in further suppression of emotions.

You may understand the concept of letting go intellectually, but don't know how to fully sequence through the body. I recognize this in my therapy work when clients encounter scenarios that mimic or remind them of the original wound and then react as they might have in the past. For example, if your mom always hovered over you and told you what to do and how to do it, you may be reactive to anyone's offer of help. If you were missing approval and attention as a child, you may continue to constantly seek that from others. You may have been in a car accident years ago and still feel anxious every time you get in a car. We continue to circle around what is not fully resolved from our past. **Time does not heal all wounds.**

These unprocessed emotions are held in the body and have been identified as driving many physical conditions.

The purpose of this book is to bring together the wisdom of letting go and the wisdom of the body. The body is an incredible resource and can support us in our path to freedom. Whether letting go of thoughts, feelings, habits, relationships or sensations, the body is available as an ally and can lead the way. **Where the body goes, the mind will follow.** The body holds unprocessed emotions that the mind may not have any memory of. Simple practices like changing posture, softening the shoulders, taking a step toward or away from something, or someone, can provide a wealth of information that may not be available through thinking or even mindfulness practices. Putting the body into movement allows hidden emotions to surface and move and release in ways that can be difficult for the mind to imagine. When I let my body lead, it reminds me of patterns that became established in my body when I was a child. I can feel the shrinking that happened when I was told I was "too much" or "too exuberant" and the pulling away that I experienced when I was blamed (innocent or not). Letting myself be consciously present with these habitual movement patterns, I can lean into them, release them and find a new way of moving. When I move differently, my mind also works differently. More options are available.

Letting go is an act of giving up—giving up to Spirit all that does not serve our highest good. But it's not an act of giving up in the way most tend to think. It is not apathy and does not mean that action is unnecessary. Sometimes action is necessary. Letting go moves whatever is in the way of action out of the way.

Our thoughts can be in the way of action, especially if we think we're not good enough, not deserving and not capable. Thoughts like these become erroneously instilled and embodied in childhood and greatly decrease the likelihood of taking actions that are in our highest good as adults.

Emotions can also be troublemakers if we hang on to them and don't let them complete their natural cycles. We might feel that our anger is justified or serving us, or that our grief is loyalty and will never move, so we hold on. But taking action while angry is not as powerful or effective as moving through anger and finding our strong, centered voice. People don't tend to hear us or take us seriously when we say "No!" from anger. Likewise, we can hold on to grief for longer than necessary, thinking grief is the only way to stay connected to the one we've lost. We forget that we can also remember through joy and love. Holding on to grief for too long can, over time, create a wall that cuts us off from feeling love completely.

Habits such as worry and procrastination can also sabotage our lives. Both these habits tend to be accompanied by resistance—"Don't worry" and "Stop being so lazy" are common things we say to ourselves and may also hear from others. These can be fun to play with and put into motion.

Both comments reinforce resistance and feeling bad about ourselves and our behavior. Instead, if we consciously let ourselves resist and maybe even push back, there's an opportunity for habits to shift.

Another area worth exploring in terms of how the body and movement can support us is the realm of goals and success. For example, if we're hesitant to get into action, taking a small physical step can open doors internally. If we can acknowledge and move with the fears of actually achieving the goal, we may receive new information that supports forward movement or possibly deciding to let the goal dissolve. We may even discover it was never really what we wanted to begin with.

Feelings of stuckness or lack of motivation are not uncommon in my therapy practice. This is an area where allowing the body even minute movements can have an enormous impact. Finding the places that are not stuck and tapping into excitement and fun, rather than the "have to" and pressure that many live with, can change the experience dramatically.

The applications and opportunities for movement are limitless.

Most would agree we are living in a rather fragile and unsteady world. **When our internal world is also unsteady, we have less ability to successfully navigate the challenges of the external world. The world needs centered people now.** People who can access strength and wisdom as needed. When we let go of personal holdbacks, we can access and connect to the love and wisdom that is our true nature. From a steady place, we are better equipped to take the action necessary to transform the world. When I feel grounded and centered, I can support others in feeling grounded and centered. When I recognize my needs as important and learn how to internally respond to them, I'm not looking to others to take care of me. And when I witness injustice in the world, I can feel my strength and take appropriate action.

Our true nature is one of curiosity, wonder, joy and love and is constantly evolving. And the experience of life doesn't have to be as hard as we make it. When we let go, we have more access to fun, creativity, connection and all that we are. And the body knows the way. Where the body goes, the mind will follow. **Let's (let) go!**

CHAPTER 1

LETTING GO IS A SPIRITUAL PRACTICE

WHAT IS SPIRITUALITY

Spirituality is a term that covers a broad range of experiences. Each person's definition is unique, but most would agree it involves a connection to something greater than oneself, whether that be a higher power, nature, or community.

From the Oxford dictionary, spirituality is the quality of being concerned with the human spirit or soul as opposed to material or physical things.

For me, it's the experience of remembering the truth of who I am. And that means letting go of everything that blocks that awareness. **When caught in the humanness of desire, we can lose track of the love and joy that is our essence.**

Almost every spiritual practice asks us to surrender and let go. The book *A Course in Miracles* offers such lessons as "I could see peace instead of this", and "I loose the world from all I thought it was", and "I am not a body, I am free."[1] These lessons and others ask us to break our identification with egoic thinking, to recognize how we are always projecting onto others what we think and feel and to recognize we are more than the body.

In *Living Untethered,* Michael Singer writes, "You get lost in the objects of consciousness, instead of focusing on the source of consciousness."[2] We get caught in a thought or feeling and don't recognize it as separate from ourselves. We use language such as "I am angry" or "I am sad" as if that is all we are instead of noticing that we are having an experience. Spiritual awakening is about untangling consciousness from the objects of consciousness. **Letting go is how we become untangled.**

When I facilitate *Life Between Lives* sessions (where we visit with friends and guides in the space between lifetimes), clients are often told by guides and elders to let go.[3] They are advised to let go of experiences, people, feelings, beliefs, guilt and shame. In one session, a client was told she had "insufficient information" regarding another person's actions. In truth, **we are often dealing with "insufficient information" about life.** But the mind has a strong urge to know everything and believes it does! To that end, it makes stuff up. And all that made-up stuff becomes justification for holding on.

HOW LETTING GO SUPPORTS FREEDOM

While in a body on Earth, people naturally tend to be wrapped up in themselves. What arises in our body-mind draws the most attention. We need multiple practices that support and remind us of the love and joy that is our true nature. The ability to let go is an invaluable tool on the path to freedom.

Lester Levinson, the originator of *The Sedona Method,* said, "You must want freedom more than you want to make the world real."[4]

I've come back to these words and this concept many times since first hearing them years ago. As a concept, "Letting go of wanting to make the world real" includes a willingness to loosen our grip on our beliefs, feelings, attachments and aversions. And some days I do want freedom more than anything, and other days I want the husband, the dog, the house and more. And sometimes I have the wisdom to recognize that freedom doesn't have to exclude these things.

Can we have everything we want and still be spiritual? Ironically, I believe the answer lies in letting go of wanting. Of letting go of any attachment or aversion to how life unfolds. Many practices teach letting go of attachment, fewer teach letting go of aversion. But both attachment and aversion keep us hooked to lack. When we want something, we are affirming that we do not have it. In some ways, it's the opposite of gratitude, denying what we do have. Regarding aversion, the Buddhist saying "what you resist, persists" speaks to its power. **Resistance is an energy force, with the energy being directed toward what we don't want.** And rather than being effective in pushing away what we don't want (whether it be a person, thing or emotion), the resistance keeps us in that experience. You might even remember trying to avoid someone and running into them repeatedly, or being upset about construction noise outside that gets louder in response to your upset. This is resistance in action. Both aversion and attachment are our companions on the journey of life.

As we let go of the human desires, attachments, aversions, beliefs, emotions and sensations that keep us identifying (only) as the body-mind, we remember our true nature more and more often. We find a path to living with compassion. It doesn't mean we don't feel. We may feel more because of letting go. We may feel heartbreak for human conditions and others going through challenging times or experiencing challenging lives. We trust ourselves to feel these things, to move through those feelings and come back to peace. Being conscious and aware of what's moving through us, being with it and letting it go, shifts us internally. We become lighter and more open to the rhythms of the universe. And a side effect of being more receptive and open could be receiving the things the personality wants. As previously mentioned, I absolutely believe in a benevolent universe, one that wants us to have what we want, if it is in our own and others' highest interests.

BODY AS COMPANION

The body is our companion on our spiritual journey. We could think of the body as home to a sacred passenger. The sacred passenger becomes one with its home during the journey, integrating with the body in the best way possible for the tasks at hand. Sometimes the sacred passenger has chosen a challenging vehicle (the body may feel too sensitive, too impulsive, too big, too small) and thoughts may arise about the inadequacy of the body-vehicle. But often, the lessons we come to learn are connected to the body's wiring. Maybe the lesson is about having more compassion for oneself and others or learning to stand up for oneself. To that end, maybe your body has more struggles than others or your spine is a weak or strong component of your body. Your highly sensitive body does more than create allergic responses

4

to foods you love or find loud noises highly agitating. Your highly sensitive body probably supports your intuition and relationships. It may alert you to issues that others overlook. Seeing what others are often oblivious to could be your superpower.

What strengths or weaknesses in your body are you aware of and working with? What strengths or weaknesses in your body have you been judging or ignoring?

And what about the possibility that our life plan (blueprint) is embedded in the body? What if the answers to so many of our questions are already with us in our cellular system? It's not that farfetched. Think about palm reading and the belief that the size, shape and lines on a person's palm and fingers mirror their individuality and life path, including whom they might be compatible with.[5] We live in an infinite universe, with infinite possibilities. Who's to say what's real or made up?

An open mind full of wonder and curiosity supports every practice in this book and most experiences you encounter daily.

PRACTICES FOR CONNECTING

For almost all of us, being in a human body and living life involves some amnesia about all that exists beyond the body-mind. The practices in this chapter can be used any time you find yourself wrapped up in daily activity, thoughts, and feelings, and forgetting that you are more than these experiences.

PRACTICE #1: COCOON YOURSELF

The human experience is strongly centered around what we call "me" or "I". Despite what we say, we're usually most focused on our own needs and desires. This doesn't make us selfish; it reveals our humanity. When we start acting as if others should also consider our needs the most important we are entering selfish or narcissistic behavior.

For this practice, wrap yourself up into a tightly wound ball and notice how it feels to pay attention only to yourself. Have fun with this for a while and then let yourself slowly unwind and see what you experience when not so tightly wound. Play with going back and forth, enjoying both the opening, expansive experience and the closed, pulled-in experience.

PRACTICE #2: WANTING

Allow yourself to think about something you've been wanting. It can be a material thing, it can be acknowledgment or connection, anything at all. Notice what you feel in your body while focused on that desire. And then, imagine not wanting it. Being okay without it. Again, what happens to your body? Keep going back and forth, paying particular attention to sensation. Do you feel light, heavy, warm, tingly, shaky, open? (To name a few of the words we can use to describe sensation.) Most people tend to feel more open and available when they let go of wanting. But sometimes, it brings up fear or other emotions. Noticing what's happening in the body can help you identify hidden feelings. (We play more with wanting as a habit in Chapter 7 and in relationship to goals in Chapter 9.)

PRACTICE #3: REMEMBER CONNECTION

Allow yourself to remember a time when you felt connected to something bigger than yourself. You may have been out in nature or sitting in your grandmother's lap, or your meditation chair. It doesn't matter what you call it; what matters is the feeling of connection. This type of connection involves no clinging. Allow yourself to remember what that felt like. Perhaps you're aware of feeling lighter, more joyous or peaceful. Let yourself stay with this feeling of openness and expansion, paying attention to what you're experiencing in your body. When we feel connected, we tend to feel more relaxed. See if your shoulders and neck have softened, or if your breathing has steadied or your stomach has relaxed. When you can identify the sensations that accompany connection, you can use those references to tap into the experience. Loosening your shoulders and neck, steadying your breathing, and softening your stomach will help you access the relaxed feelings of connection. *Where the body goes, the mind will follow.* Recognizing that you can find connection through the body at any time is an important resource in your toolbox.

CHAPTER 2
BASICS OF LETTING GO

WHY WE HOLD ON

There are probably as many reasons we hold on as there are people on the planet. It's a highly individualized activity with some central themes.

We hold tight to our beliefs because we think they define us. Or, because our parents or friends hold that belief, and we accept their beliefs without thoughtful consideration, or because we want to belong. Or because having an opinion seems important. We think we'd be lost without our beliefs and wouldn't know how to behave.

We also cling tightly to our feelings for some of the same reasons, or because we believe they are somehow protecting us. Or, that we have a right to them (which we do, of course). Or that letting go of them would be disloyal. Or because they seem so strong, stronger than our ability to release them. Maybe nobody ever taught or modeled for us how to let a feeling move.

We hold on to ways of being in the world because we don't recognize we have options. These habits have worked in the past (perhaps poorly, but so what?), and it takes effort to expand our toolkits. Many of the modes we use to interact with others are driven by internal or external expectations. For example, we may define ourselves by the work we do and the style or manner we do our jobs, then develop a belief that our worth or value is informed by our careers. Often, our belief that we need to meet others' expectations is a construct we created ourselves.

We're also attached to being right about everything. We don't like change or learning that we've invested in something that maybe isn't working out so well. And we really like to have a sense of being in control of ourselves and the world.

We hold on to resentments, worries, relationships, sensations, grief, opinions, the need to understand and to our longings and fantasies.

As mentioned earlier, you may think you need to hold on to grief to honor or remember someone, or you think you need to stay angry to hold a boundary, so you don't recreate a situation. But if you dig a little deeper, you may find you really want to hold on to the love and memories. Or, in the case of boundaries, perhaps what you really want to keep, and honor, are the lessons you've learned from people who've challenged you. Holding on to being upset doesn't support retaining the lesson. One way to shift your relationship with, or resistance to, letting go is to reframe the question and ask, "What is the payoff for holding on?"

WHY LET GO?

As with anything, when it comes to letting go, the mind wants to know, "Why should I?" And, of course, if anyone tells you that you should do something, you will likely resist. Finding your motivation to let go (or release) becomes critically important. In my personal experience and in the experience of my clients, gains and rewards from releasing have been numerous and significant. I especially enjoy witnessing clients who let go of the lifelong habit of worrying (likely because I also grew up learning to worry). Clients have reported new ease in relationships, more clarity about what they want in life, freedom from grief and anxiety, and a sense of competence in navigating emotions and reactions as they arise, all as a result of letting go.

The cost of holding on is limitation. Letting go supports more ease and options in the world.

The anger and upset we feel towards others are carried in our bodies and generally affect us much more than they affect the ones we are upset with. Unprocessed anger has also been shown to drive many physical conditions and is often lurking below depression and anxiety.

Letting go is a journey of embracing yourself. Of shedding what is not necessary, what does not support you, and ultimately, what is not authentically you. Letting go of negative self-beliefs can only support you in being more present and alive in the world.

If there's a history of extreme trauma, you may have created stories and patterns to keep yourself safe. But you now feel trapped in your history.

Letting go is a path of freedom and courage. It's also an act of service. Others in your communities can feel the ripple effect. Seeing you let go can also inspire them to let go.

Letting go helps you see possibility. It can create breathing space and a sense of peace and relaxation.

And as written on a favorite T-shirt of mine, *"Let Go, Feel Good"*!

WAYS LETTING GO HAPPENS

IN A MOMENT OR OVER A LIFETIME

Sometimes we can catch a feeling as it arises, notice it and let it go. An easy example is the agitation that might arise if someone cuts you off while driving. This doesn't need to have a lasting impact or even affect the rest of your day. You can decide at the moment to let go.

Other times, you may be working with something that has layers and layers to it. If you experienced years of abuse or even a single highly traumatizing event, there will be many components to letting go. There is likely anger (sometimes hidden), grief, associated beliefs about yourself and the world, misplaced guilt and more. You can spend years uncovering all the ways you were impacted by your past. We are incredibly clever and resourceful when it comes to covering our wounds. You may be a strong, successful businessperson, but seeking approval is still driving many of your actions and decisions because of the absence of approval when young. A car accident could also have multiple aspects to it. In these more complicated scenarios, remember to take time and get the professional support you need.

SPECIFIC VERSUS GENERAL

Sometimes we have something very specific we want to let go of, such as anger about a situation, judgment about ourselves or regret about an experience. And sometimes, we want to let go of everything that stands in the way of freedom. Often, when I'm dancing, I ask to be guided in letting go of any blockages to a particular task or of anything getting in the way of love. Give yourself permission to play with releasing in both specific and non-specific areas. The more open you can be with yourself the more likely you will discover what the real upset is and what might be blocking your ability to let go.

A LITTLE OR A LOT

In any given moment, we may be willing to let go of a tiny bit of upset or all of it. We may be willing to "think about thinking about" letting go, holding the possibility for the future. We may not feel the impact of the letting go we do during the moment but become aware of a subtle shift the next day or a week later. **Know that the practice of letting go of anything supports letting go of everything, whether we let go of a lot or a little in the moment.** I used to have a phobia of needles (and a good story to justify it). I had been practicing letting go of upsets and worries for years and then one day I faced the prospect of being poked by a needle for a blood draw. I remember saying to my husband, "This is going to take some releasing," but as the dreaded day approached, I realized fear wasn't present. This surprised me, and my lack of fear showed me that the practice of letting go was taking root in my body.

WHAT SUPPORTS LETTING GO

Some practices support letting go and some practices (like judgment) impede it. We'll look at how to work with attitude, play, wonder and imagination, deep listening, and writing to support you in your letting go journey.

ATTITUDE

Fostering curiosity, a sense of wonder, and a non-judgmental attitude toward ourselves contributes to an environment where all aspects of one's identity are embraced and permitted. We impede our path to freedom, however, by pushing away all that we believe we can't be, think or feel. All the conditions we place on ourselves keep us tightly wound and bound.

To cultivate this **attitude of allowing**, you may need to bargain with yourself. You may need to give yourself permission to judge later if you feel it necessary. Or you can say, "Let's just see what happens if I suspend judgment for ten minutes." When there's a history of judgment and expectations, even ten minutes of allowing is a giant step.

Along those lines, **give yourself credit** for the wins. Pay attention to what is shifting and acknowledge and celebrate it. The mind's tendency is to focus on what hasn't changed and what is wrong, which is not supportive of letting go. You might also be telling yourself, "This is going to be hard." In this case, I would recommend challenging that thought. Maybe it's going to be easy.

PLAY

One might describe me as a worshiper of play. I hold it sacred and believe our natural state is playful, curious and joyful. **I define play as an open, unattached way of interacting with self, others or objects—spontaneous being.** I wrote my master's thesis *Reclaiming an Adult Relationship to Play* because I think it's a travesty if we were taught to stop playing at any age.[6] Play supports letting go in that it brings us into relationship with what's right in front of us, right now. We can play with objects, with thoughts, feelings, with ideas and with others. Play allows and supports trying on new possibilities. We can make a game out of almost anything, including our upsets, our judgments, our beliefs and our relationships. In playing, we can allow what once was to break up and dissolve and come into new form. And, if we don't like the new options we've created, we can always go back to what was. Because, after all, we were *just playing*. **Play takes the pressure off.**

Many of the ways we interact in the world were initially developed through play. We tried different roles and characters, mimicking or in reaction to those in our environment. If mom was bossy, we may have decided we should be bossy like her or submissive in response to her. If dad was laid back and easygoing, but people trampled on him, that role might not be so attractive. When we lock ourselves into playing any one particular role, we have fewer options in how we interact in the world. Going back via play to the origin of the role (which has now become a part of our identity) is a powerful way to unwind and dissolve stuck patterns that once served but are no longer our best option.

WONDER AND IMAGINATION

While our minds can lead us down a path of negative thinking and contracted awareness, they are also capable of taking us outside ourselves to places far beyond.

I love and encourage **the concept and practice of wondering.** Rather than thinking I know what's going to happen, or what path I'm going to take, I **allow** myself to **wonder** what will unfold. The practice of wondering is powerful for many reasons. It allows the mind to open to possibility. When we wonder where the money will come from instead of worrying about it or trying to figure it out, we open ourselves to support from beyond the mind. Wondering also opens the creative channels of our brain. A new thought or idea might present itself. Wondering as a practice also reminds us that we don't know everything, we're not in control, and that mystery is alive and well. It supports us in stepping away from the constant need to figure everything out.

When you let yourself wonder about the unknown, it creates an opening for exploration. You know you are playing in the world of imagination where there are no right or wrong answers. You allow yourself to create things, to make things up. No one will know and no one will care what you're wondering about.

Give yourself permission to use the power of wonder and imagination interchangeably with physically moving your body as you practice the exercises in this book.

DEEP LISTENING

The practice of deep listening is often referenced as a communication tool with others. But, if you think about it, why wouldn't you cultivate it for yourself? I'm sure you want to be heard as much as anyone. It starts with being willing to really listen to yourself. **When you feel heard internally, you may find it's not that important whether others hear you or not.** Or you may find you don't want to be around people who can't hear you. Either is okay. What's important is that you start to recognize you have the ability to meet your own needs, and that's empowering.

Deep listening is a practice. It is hearing what is being spoken and not spoken. It's the ability to quiet the mind enough to hear what's under the constant chatter. Both the chatter in your mind and the chatter coming from others. It's tapping into the information that comes through sensation and energy.

Deep listening goes beyond the surface thoughts to what lies below. Below our surface thoughts are the fears and desires that ultimately drive our actions and agitation. These underlying fears and desires need to be revealed for us to effectively let them go. See Practice #6 in this chapter on how to cultivate deep listening.

WRITING SUPPORTS LETTING GO

As you play with the activities in this book, you could also start a journal or workbook. Imagine your journal as a witness to your processing and progress. Putting pen to paper in and of itself is movement and allows letting go. You may find that writing down the thoughts and feelings that you've been holding on to for some time helps them dissolve. Remember to employ the previously mentioned curiosity, wonder and non-judgmental attitudes in your journaling. Writing your insights down can reveal more insights or help anchor them. Writing has been shown to improve memory and enhance creativity. It will also serve to help you remember the shifts that are happening and counteract the mind's tendency to focus on what's not working.

BASICS OF LETTING GO PRACTICES

My older brother's high school engineering teacher was known to say, "The trouble with you guys is you don't know the basics!" Although I wasn't in the class, my brother and his friends picked up this line as a mantra, often repeating it in my presence. It's stayed with me all these years, reminding me that foundational knowledge supports all practices.

PRACTICE #4: WILLINGNESS

An attitude of willingness is critical when it comes to letting go and self-growth in any form.Shift doesn't happen because somebody else told you to do it or because you're pressuring yourself to do it. The joke: "How many therapists does it take to change a light bulb?" The answer being: "Only one, but the light bulb has to be willing to change," speaks to attitude.

Willingness is more apt to be present when you make the journey fun. Play, wonder and imagination not only support letting go, but they also support a good attitude. No need to ask which came first.

In this practice, pick a couple of things you struggle with that are ripe for exploration. It might be the feeling that nobody sees you or hears you. Or the thought that you're not allowed to voice your opinion. Or that you're not strong enough or smart enough. Most of us have plenty of material to work with.

Begin by noticing what your current experience (or perception) of not being seen or heard feels like. Or what holding in your voice looks like. What posture does your body naturally take?

And then begin asking these questions or any others that come to mind:

☞ Am I willing to be seen? Am I willing to be listened to? What would it feel like to allow myself to be seen (or heard)? How would my posture and gestures shift?

☞ What would it feel like if others actually saw me or heard me? (This is different than the above questions, which focus on your willingness to allow others to see and hear you.)

☞ What if I knew I was enough?

Pay attention to the thoughts and the feelings that arise and any shifts in body posture as you entertain these questions. You might find there are some things you are not willing to look at right now. Acknowledge them and allow for the possibility that the time is not right, and you will know when it is.

Letting go of anything supports letting go of everything. How willing are you to let go of everything? Becoming aware of what you are and what you are not willing to let go of, and how much, without judgment, will help guide your journey.

PRACTICE #5: PLAY, WONDER AND IMAGINATION

It's unfortunate that we need to remember to play, and for many, how to play. But here we are. Wonder and imagination are inherent in play and can also be independent activities. There are many playful practices employing wonder and play to follow in all the chapters, but as a warmup, try some of the following:

- Use senses as play signals (e.g. every time you hear the phone ring, you shimmy)
- Dance to the music as if you were a rock star
- Write a silly rhyming poem
- Build a sculpture from items on your desk or food in your cupboard
- Bounce in your seat and wonder about what you might be shaking loose
- Play hide-and-seek with the dog
- Borrow your kid's toys and remember being a child (remember to return them!)
- Skip around the house imagining you are a lemur or a magpie (yes, they are both known as skippers!)
- Get on the swings at the playground

PRACTICE #6: CULTIVATE DEEP LISTENING

In order to be able to truly listen to both self and other, we first need to get past the constant chatter of the mind. Many new and prospective clients tell me they overthink and overanalyze but haven't considered they could change this. This practice is about developing the skill to listen to yourself and your body. You will find that this subsequently improves your ability to listen to others.

This is a five-step process that could take minutes or days to complete each time you go through it. The more you do it, the more it will become part of how you go through life.

1. Bring attention to the habit of being driven by thoughts. Maybe you notice that you've missed what you were reading or listening to. Maybe you have the experience of spending hours planning a party and forgetting to enjoy it. Or you miss miles and miles of stunning scenery because of preoccupation with thoughts. Bringing awareness (without judgment) to being caught up in thinking allows space for shifts to happen.

2. Decide to practice a new behavior. Something small. You won't change getting pulled into the mind in one day. Maybe you choose to bring more awareness to your breathing or plan a daily (or hourly) check-in with yourself.

3. Start catching the behavior of overthinking in the moment and consciously choose not to engage with the thought(s);

instead, become aware of sensation. What are you hearing, sensing and feeling?

4.   Don't try to figure out what you are hearing, sensing and feeling. Just open to the sensations and see what you learn. Or already knew and may have been ignoring.

5.   Give some attention to what you are discovering by noticing sensation. You may find something physical, such as hunger, fatigue or pain. Or you may notice there's a feeling of disappointment, sadness or anger that you've been ignoring. When you know what's really here, you can effectively take the next step toward letting go or moving forward.

PRACTICE #7: FREE WRITING

You may already be familiar with the practice of free writing. If you're new to the concept, here are the rules: no editing, no punctuation, no judging, no censoring. Put your pen (or pencil or crayon or charcoal) to paper and just start writing. You can decide what length of time you are going to write for or not. Allow an unfiltered stream of consciousness (it's happening all the time anyway) and see what shows up.

CHAPTER 3

HOW THE BODY SUPPORTS LETTING GO

Our education is sorely bereft of what I consider basic life skills. Relationships with self and body are high on that list. When we don't know how to be in a relationship with the body we inhabit, when we don't know how to listen, when we don't know how to rest, how to trust and meet our own needs, we go looking for others to meet these needs. And, no matter how they try, they will never be as good at it as we can be.

In the well-known song "*Let There Be Peace on Earth*," the words "and let it begin with me" are often thought to mean that peace begins with our acts of kindness toward others.[7] We must first recognize and cultivate peace within ourselves before we can offer it to others. When at peace with yourself, you are much less likely to "go to war" with others. And if called to confront or "go to war" with others, it will be intentional and grounded.

EMOTIONS IN THE BODY

We feel emotions in the body, and we store unprocessed emotions (those we were unable or unwilling to be with) in the body. Potentially in every cell. I like to think we put them there for safekeeping until we can process and release them in a safe environment. Did you know that we have a bounty of emotional receptor sites in the belly? When you say "I have a gut feeling," that's no joke. When you get an "intuitive hit," what are you aware of in the body? If you are not aware, it can be fun to start paying attention.

Sensation in the body is different from thinking. **While we can think about the past or future, we can only feel what's present right now. Simply paying attention to sensation is a spiritual practice, in that it connects us to the present moment.**

Getting in touch with what's moving inside of you and letting it find its external expression, allows for release and shift. When you put sensation into movement in your body, you quite literally have been moved, changed and transformed. When you feel the shove you want to give your spouse, anger can release. When you feel the reach toward what you desire, lust can sequence into action.

The body is our ally. When we start listening, we may become aware of fatigue before we get sick; we may catch the gut's warning to leave a situation; and we might identify the pain in our neck to be a recurring reaction to someone. All these experiences in the body can inform appropriate action.

LEARNING TO LISTEN TO THE BODY

While the language of movement and letting go is second nature to me, it might feel like a foreign language to you. But I promise this is a language your body knows. You knew it before you spoke words. Your body still knows the language, even if your mind needs a reminder.

MEET YOURSELF WHERE YOU ARE

This is not a concept you were likely taught in school. Starting with the basics, the ability to meet yourself where you are must begin with knowing where that is. Certainly, being aware of your external environment is a component of this, but it is the internal environment we want to be curious about. In Michael Singer's book, *Living Untethered*, he writes, "You get to the point where you realize all you're ever doing in there is trying to be okay."[2] Most of us don't stop to check what's actually going on "in there" very often. In almost every practice offered in this book, getting in touch first with what's happening inside will allow a more powerful release.

KNOW THAT ALL MOVEMENT IS MEDICINE

If you just set people in motion they'll heal themselves.

Gabrielle Roth[8]

Most know the importance of movement for good physical health. Circulation, sleep, digestion, mobility and other physical functions are improved by keeping the body moving. Studies also regularly cite movement as an antidote to depression, anxiety, stress and various mental health issues. And of course, I agree. All movement is good movement.

But the practice of conscious movement? That's the juicy stuff. Many established movement practices (Yoga, Tai Chi, Pilates, 5Rhythms®,

Soul Motion and more) fall under the umbrella of conscious movement. **But even walking across the street with an awareness of your steps is conscious movement.** In dance, we follow how the body wants to move, rather than telling it what steps to take. The range of movement accepted in society is a fraction of what the body is capable of. When you let the body lead, it can take you to places in your mind and beyond your mind that were previously inaccessible or hidden from awareness.

A STEP-BY-STEP GUIDE TO GETTING ACQUAINTED WITH YOUR BODY

☞ Step 1—Breathe and observe your breath as it moves through the body. Notice the obvious (chest rising, stomach expanding) and the not so obvious (mouth, face, throat).

☞ Step 2—Bring attention to areas in your body you weren't aware of in Step 1 (head, shoulders, feet and toes, for example).

☞ Step 3—Imagine oxygen flowing into these areas (focusing on those areas as you breathe in and out, sending them a little extra air).

☞ Step 4—Pay attention to what feels tight, what feels loose, what feels numb.

☞ Step 5—Become aware of any physical pain or discomfort.

☞ Step 6—Become aware of any emotional upset or agitation.

☞ Step 7—Say "Hello!" This might feel like a conversation with a new acquaintance or learning a new language. Pat yourself on the back, rub a tender area, give your body some verbal reassurance and ask any questions that arise.

UNIVERSAL BODY PRACTICES

These practices are relevant to all aspects of life and most topics in this book.

PRACTICE #8: PUT THE BODY INTO MOTION

No thinking, no introspection, no trying to figure out what to do. Just put on some music and let your body move. Shake, shimmy, stomp, bounce, twirl and do any or all the things that came naturally when you were three years old.

PRACTICE #9: PUT THE FEELING INTO MOVEMENT

Feelings are designed to move. Much like waves on the ocean they have a beginning, middle and end. They can be very subtle or big and loud. But the waves complete when they hit land. There may be some splash back, but they will complete. And waves do this of their own accord, as will the feelings that arise in you if they are allowed to move. Movement of feelings is impeded by beliefs of what's allowed or that feelings indicate weakness, the fear of becoming stuck in a feeling, thoughts connected to taking care of others, and concerns about what others might think. You may have been told boys don't cry, girls don't get angry, or don't be too happy or any number of things people say about feelings. **Reclaiming the full range of emotions is critical to**

personal freedom. Our work is to have the capacity to allow a full range of life to move within us and around us.

Can you be curious about how your anger would move if allowed? What would a sad dance look like and feel like in your body? What direction would courage or fear move in?

Allow yourself to play with all the options that come to mind. Bring back the wonder of your 4-year-old self or the daring of your 12-year-old self. Your imagination is yours to use in any way you want to and can be a powerful ally in moving stuck emotions. And you might even want to get up and move what you're imagining.

PRACTICE #10: MOVE WITH THE MUSCLES

The muscles are the workhorse of the body with some of their major tasks being locomotion, lifting and pushing. They are in charge of giving birth and pumping blood. They help us sustain posture, fall into or crawl or leap out of bed, and brush our teeth. Muscle tissue communicates directly with the brain and chemical interactions. A body that exercises regularly has better communication with the brain. The brain is designed for both stimulating and receiving feedback from movement!

Exploring your relationship with the muscles can have many distinct aspects and associated feelings. Maybe you're okay with using your legs to deliver a good kick, but punching someone with your arm feels scary or repulsive. Are you allowed to reach for what you want? Push against what you don't want? Muscles are especially important in setting boundaries. If you can't find what a strong "no" feels like in your body, it will be challenging to find conviction when saying "no" to others.

Muscles also come into play with giving and receiving. While this topic can arise as it relates to goals (and will be visited in that chapter), it's also pertinent to relationships. How can you be in a healthy relationship with another if you only know how to give? Or do you only know how to take? We need to be comfortable with both giving and receiving to feel good about our relationships with others.

Some things to ponder—**Do you tend to muscle through life? To be overly dependent on physical strength? Do you push back against the inevitable? Do you think you're weak because your muscles are not developed?**

Our relationship with our muscles is literally and figuratively a relationship with balance. Can I bend when needed? Can I push forward? Can I give and receive? If the purpose of being in a human body is to learn to be okay with everything, the muscles are, by necessity, a foundational practice.

Allow yourself to become aware of the muscles in your body. Start with the familiar ones such as biceps and triceps (arms) and quadriceps and hamstrings (legs). Feel the tightness, the flexibility, the strength and the weakness of each muscle. Pretend that you're meeting it for the first time and be curious about the different ways it moves. When you feel ready, become curious about the muscles in your face—the ones that move your mouth into a smile or a frown, the ones that open and close your eyes and the muscles involved in sneezing. The human body has over 650 muscles (the exact number varies based on groupings by scientists). How many can you locate and consciously move?

PRACTICE #11: MOVE WITH THE JOINTS

The joints are part of the skeletal system, the connection points between the bones relative to each other. Some joints provide structural support and don't move at all. (Those that hold your skull in place, for example.) And other joints are all about flexibility and mobility. Bending, rotating, extending and directional changes are all dependent on the joints. **Joints equate to flexibility and options in the body and life experiences.** The joints contribute to your ability to change course, adjust to circumstances and overcome obstacles.

Allow yourself to explore the movement of your wrists, your elbows, your fingers, your knees, hips, neck, jaw and ankles (just a few of the 360 joints in the body). As you explore, pay attention to how the joints move (forward, back, up, down, around) and what feels fluid, stiff, achy or even cranky. Notice if any thoughts or feelings arise as you move your hips or roll your ankle. Every part of the body holds feelings and memories, and even gentle movements can awaken these.

PRACTICE #12: BE A SKELETON

The skeleton on its own, without the support of the other systems, is loosey-goosey, relaxed and unperturbed. Bones can support a sense of steadiness and calm and can allow us to be "easygoing."[9] Most of us could use more bone-driven experiences.

Let yourself soften your muscles and relax your joints. Imagine going a little loosey-goosey, a little spacey. As you settle, you may become more aware of the skeletal system. Focusing this time on the bones without the support of the muscles. The bones may want to shake, stretch, jiggle or collapse. You may begin to feel a little more relaxed and settled into yourself; if not, do it again. It may be exactly what you are most in need of.

PRACTICE #13: CHANGE PERSPECTIVE

The way we engage and perceive the world is based on perspective. Every person has a different perspective, yet almost everyone believes their perspective is the right and only one. Whether you are working to change a negative self-belief, move through old feelings of resentment, or feel stymied in achieving your goals, a new perspective can be somewhat helpful or transformational.

This can be a simple practice done wherever you are. It might even be one you want to start consciously doing in any meeting that has become boring or contentious.

Allow yourself to look to your left. Take in your surroundings. What do you see, feel, hear, sense as you look to your left? What are you aware of internally and externally? (If in a meeting, do others' voices get louder, softer, sound different?) When you feel ready, look to your right. What do you see, feel, hear, sense as you look to your right? What are you aware of internally and externally?

If you're in a space with a window, shift your awareness between what's happening inside and what's happening outside. This practice of going back and forth between two different focuses allows each to soften and, simultaneously, expands awareness of other perspectives and options. You can also sway your attention by bringing your awareness inside yourself, then shifting your awareness to others. These practices will support your ability to shift focus more effortlessly in all areas of your life.

PRACTICE #14: SOFTEN AND OPEN

It's not uncommon to not know what you're feeling, physically or emotionally, at any given moment. Or you may know you feel a little off but haven't identified that you were triggered by something someone said to you twenty minutes ago. And sometimes, an emotion has already subsided, but you're still telling stories about the upset (keeping it alive with the retelling). You also might not recognize how often you are resisting your current experience. Every time you want something to be different than the way it is, every time you want someone to be or behave differently, every time you say "I hate the wind" or the cold or the heat, resistance is involved. And we all do it, all the time.

The practice of softening and opening is the body's way of becoming aware of internal experiences. Sometimes you may let go as you soften, sometimes you may just become more aware.

Whether you think you know how to soften or not, **trust that your body knows.** Give yourself the suggestion to soften, or soften and open, and see what happens. You could add words like melt, or dissolve, or any word that supports the process and see what your body responds to.

Contrary to what many believe, tightening the body does not keep you safe. Tightening the body also causes more shallow breathing, depriving you of important fuel for every cell. Softening and opening puts you more in touch with your center and your strength, which will allow you to navigate the world with more awareness and confidence.

CHAPTER 4
BELIEFS AND THINKING

BELIEFS ARE NOT FACTS

It's common to encounter situations where friends or family members recount the same event with differing perspectives. Or perhaps you once believed something happened for a certain reason, only to find out later you were totally off track. Or perhaps you used to believe something about yourself or another that you no longer hold true.

This happens to all of us, but somehow, we still operate as if our beliefs are facts. We don't like it when others challenge our beliefs, and we are drawn to others who think like we do. All is well and good, until it's not. Our world is divided based on beliefs. Wars are fought because of who or what we choose to worship or because we think differently about what is right and wrong. **Decisions about what to do with our lives are based on what we think of ourselves. And sometimes we are wrong.**

Many of our core beliefs arose when we were young and are a product of what we were told and shown about ourselves. In a loving, supportive environment it's likely that a positive self-image was formed. Whereas if raised in a less than loving household, you may believe "you don't deserve" or that "you're not good enough." If you consider how a different environment might have formed a completely distinct set of beliefs, it's worth wondering if your beliefs are founded in any truth at all. And while I mentioned a straightforward example (loving vs. not loving), it's considerably more complicated than that. I've worked with clients who were raised by self-involved parents and subsequently developed beliefs that they were not deserving of attention. And clients that had problematic siblings and took the path of being the good, perfect child with an accompanying belief, "don't be a bother." Or alcoholism fostered a belief that the world is unsafe, and people are untrustworthy.

We take on beliefs of others to feel connected or safe. We also do the opposite; not believing what others believe because we want nothing to do with them. A fun little exercise might be to spend a day or two questioning your thoughts. Simply ask yourself, "Why do I believe that?" and see what you notice. Of course, you will only catch a few of the thousands and thousands of thoughts you have each day, but that's more than enough.

We have developed points of view about everything under the sun and beyond. Thoughts about the best diet, how much money we need, what happens after death, what constitutes correct moral thinking and behavior, how smart or stupid we and others are, and so on and so on. And we tend to rely on these beliefs often without ever pondering other possibilities.

Thinking in general can be problematic. The desire to know what and why is strong in most people. Knowing provides a false sense of control and security. If we know why something happened to someone else, we can explain and justify why it will never happen to us. Or we think if we know why we did something silly in the past, it will prevent us from ever doing it again. **We think we can solve all our problems in the mind. If that were true, many of our current problems would have been long gone.**

Beliefs are fickle and letting go of them can be challenging. After all, we've survived as long as we have believing what we do. Even negative self-beliefs serve a purpose. If you believe you're incapable, it gives you a reason not to try. If you are sure you are undeserving, that could make you feel better about not having. Sometimes, beliefs support the underlying goals. If you really like alone time, you might justify it with the perception that people don't want you around. The mind would rather have a reason (even if it's not kind or supportive or true) than not know. More than anything, the mind hates not knowing.

ATTACHMENT AND AVERSION

Both attachment and aversion give our thoughts more power. Whether we think a thought is meaningful and important or stupid and useless, the more intensely we react to that thought, the stronger the hold it has on us.

Another aspect of navigating thoughts is the impact that new age thinking has had on many. Jody came for therapy some years ago because of a skin issue. She had already come to believe the condition was driven by stress. Pretty quickly in our sessions we came upon a major internal stressor. She had learned that she was only allowed to think positive thoughts, but was continuing to experience thoughts that did not fall into the positive category and was unconsciously but loudly punishing herself for having them. If you have a positive mindset, that's great, but trying to force it upon yourself will never work. Thoughts of all flavors arise, and our work is to let them come and go without holding on or pushing them away. Some have been told that without beliefs there can be no motivation. Instead, we could consider being motivated by passion, fun and curiosity, which tap us into the creative nature of the universe.

Everything we experience is informed by what we believe. We see the world through our individual filter. On a surface layer, think of the time you bought a red convertible and all you saw on the road for weeks were red convertibles. Or you decided it was time to adopt a puppy and suddenly puppies were everywhere. We filter the world through our experiences and our thoughts about those experiences. We look for evidence to support our beliefs. When we think the world is a loving place, we are more apt to be aware of acts of kindness. If our primary assumptions are that the world is unsafe and terrifying, we will notice all the scary events happening in the world. We really want to be right, and our minds will find evidence to make it so. If you want to make your world a more enjoyable place, changing your thoughts and perceptions could go a long way.

Exploring where your beliefs and perceptions come from, wondering if they are true and if they are serving you is a journey in and of itself, and also informs much of what follows in this book. The suggestions in this section are about inviting curiosity about what you believe, trying different options, and consciously deciding if you want to continue to believe what you've always believed (and you might) or if something else might serve you a little better.

BELIEFS AND THINKING PRACTICES

While the practices in this chapter are directed at thinking and beliefs, you might also notice that they could also help with habits or emotions or relationships. Perfect. Allow yourself to adapt and adjust both the practices and their applications.

PRACTICE #15: CHANGE YOUR POSTURE

Most know that it's possible to tell how someone else is feeling through their body posture. Before the onslaught of cell phones and their accompanying slumped-over position, when we saw a friend or co-worker looking down with shoulders hunched, we would ask what was wrong.

When the same person walked by smiling or pumping their fists, it was clear they were happy. What we don't recognize is that it goes both ways: **Our thoughts and feelings affect our posture and prolonged periods of time in any posture will affect our thoughts and feelings.** Shifting your posture can support changing your beliefs.

When aware of a negative self-belief, such as *I'm not good enough*, or *I don't know how*, allow yourself to take note of the posture that goes along with the belief. It's likely contracted or pulled inward in some way. Let yourself fully go into that posture and make note of any feelings that accompany it. When you're ready, shift to a slightly more open position. Notice what changes in sensation, thought and feeling as you shift your body position. Memories might come to mind of when you were good enough or you did know how. It's also possible memories will come to mind of someone telling you that you were doing a lousy job. Just keep allowing whatever comes up. Some incidents will let go quickly; others will inform the next belief to work with. And some recalled events or thoughts will soften slightly.

Keep playing with the new, mildly more open posture for a week, paying attention to any loosening or any added information that may be revealed. When you feel like there's been a shift, try opening a little more, or standing a little taller and continue the exploration. Take your time and go slowly if something big is being revealed. It needs space to integrate.

PRACTICE #16: BOUNCE YOUR BODY AND YOUR THOUGHTS

There is compelling evidence for shaking as a way to move trauma and release stress. Animals shake after surviving attacks, and shaking has been shown to bring cortisol (stress hormone) levels down. Shaking can reprogram physical, mental and emotional holding patterns. I also learned with experience that it's really hard to hold on to a thought while bouncing.

If dealing with intrusive and repetitive thoughts, watch them for a moment and notice the impact on your body and mood. And then allow yourself to start bouncing. Big or little, sitting or standing.

What happens when you allow your body to jiggle? You will likely have more difficulty tracking thoughts. Watch the tendency to go looking for them, because as much as you may want to be free from thinking, there's a part of you that may want to hold on. If so, keep bouncing.

If you are in a meeting or a place where you don't feel comfortable doing out-of-the-ordinary things with your body, it also works to imagine bouncing the thoughts in your head. Perhaps there's a trampoline for them to roll and rebound on. Allow yourself to have fun imagining how the thoughts would flip and fall and roll while bouncing.

If necessary, or it feels like fun, add some music to bounce to. "Love Shack" by the B-52's works for me.[10] Are you bouncing yet?

PRACTICE #17: SWIRL THE THOUGHTS—AND YOUR BODY

Similar to Practice #16, bouncing thoughts, you can also swirl or imagine swirling thoughts. Do some head rolls while thinking about sending the thoughts from side to side. With swirling, you can change the speed and space of the swirl. Perhaps putting the thoughts on a merry-go-round, one thought per horse, and watching the thoughts go up and down and round and round. Or in your mind's eye, you might see the thoughts as a separate entity spinning and whirling as the dervishes do. The Islamic Sufi ritual of self-pivoting, known as whirling, is a meditation practice that supports quieting the mind.

This is also a great practice if you recognize thoughts are already swirling in your head. Leaning into what's already happening, without resisting, will allow the thoughts to soften and shift.

PRACTICE #18: STEP AWAY FROM THE MIND

We can become so caught in thinking that we don't even recognize our thoughts have captured us. (We started exploring this in the deep listening Practice #6 in Chapter 2.) But you might notice, at any moment, that your neck and shoulders feel tight, or that you're holding your breath. Or wrinkling your brow. There may be an accompanying thought about needing to focus and concentrate.

Whether you are caught by one thought in particular, or thinking in general, or obsessing on something you'd rather not be thinking about, and that thought doesn't serve you to stay focused on, it can be helpful to take a step away from yourself. Literally take a step back from where you're standing and imagine you can watch yourself thinking. Perhaps you can begin a conversation with yourself about the thought. Wonder where that thought came from, whose thought it is anyway and if you must believe it.

If you're overthinking a situation, stepping away can also help you to see that you're not getting anywhere with thinking it to death. Maybe imagine another step back. From a distance, you can have compassion for yourself and maybe even say, "There, there, sweetie, how about we take a little break?"

This practice can help you remember that you are not your thoughts, that they come and go and you can choose what to pay attention to.

PRACTICE #19: BE ALL THE THINGS

Most of us learned from our caretakers how to behave in the world. What behavior is expected and what behavior is not allowed. What we learned, observed and absorbed gets translated into beliefs about ourselves that we can notice if we step outside their parameters. Often, even well-meant interventions by our parents get translated into a complete system of thoughts. For example, maybe you didn't want to share your food or your toy with your sibling (which, by the way, there are times developmentally when being selfish is exactly what you should be supported in doing), and you were accused of being selfish. You may have taken this one incident and made it into a standard—"Selfishness is bad." And then when you perceive others as being selfish you feel judgmental. Sound familiar? It's what we do. What we do not allow in ourselves, we do not accept in others. You may also have learned you cannot be mean, lazy, judgmental or crabby. But guess what? **Sometimes, we are all those things. Whether we show it to the outside world or not.**

Permitting yourself to be selfish for an hour, judging people like crazy for ten minutes, or in your mind's eye, being as mean as they come, will allow the energy to move. You might even combine this with Practice #15 and assume the posture that goes with selfishness, being judgmental, mean, crabby or lazy. Maybe you cross your arms or frown and wrinkle your forehead when judging. Selfishness might be turning your back or stomping your feet. Or think of a cartoon character that represents those qualities and be that character. Cruella de Vil or Tony the Tiger might have something to teach you.

PRACTICE #20: TURN THE THOUGHTS INTO BUTTERFLIES

Imagine the negative or stuck thought as a butterfly (or hummingbird, dragonfly or lightning bug) and let it flit and fly around. Let yourself flap your wings (arms) fast and slow. Let yourself go slow, speed up, pause and so on. Imagine it moving in a small space and then let it expand outward. Play with changing the colors on the butterfly. Let it be dark, light, iridescent, rainbow colored.

And pay attention to what shifts in you. Perhaps you are no longer wrinkling your forehead, maybe your shoulders are relaxing and maybe you are noticing you don't have to listen to that thought.

PRACTICE #21: LET GO OF DEFENDING YOUR THOUGHTS

Because we feel so identified with our thoughts, we are in the habit of defending them, even if we don't like them. We justify and explain why we think the way we do, and that adds energy and strength to our thoughts. This goes along with looking for evidence to support our beliefs. The tendency can occur independently of others. We spend plenty of time justifying our thoughts to ourselves.

Imagine yourself in a boxing match and your thoughts are a precious object behind you. Feel the movement of protecting and defending and fighting off your opponent. And notice how much energy this takes and how much more attached you feel to your thoughts. And then, drop your arms, step aside and imagine saying to your opponent,

"Here, you can have them." Wouldn't it be lovely if we could give some of our thoughts away?

PRACTICE #22: FOCUS ELSEWHERE

When caught in a thought, we are pulled into our own world. Returning to one of the universal practices in Chapter 3, you can shift your focus to help step out of repetitive thoughts. Pausing to look out and see what's happening outside of you may serve to remind you there is a lot more going on in the world than what you are thinking. You can play with this by oscillating your attention—first become aware of what you're thinking and then become aware of what's happening externally, going back and forth for a while. You might want to drop your head to your chest as you go inward and lift your head as you notice what's beyond. You can even wonder what others might be thinking about. And it's probably not you or what you're thinking.

PRACTICE #23: TURN YOUR THOUGHTS INTO A SILLY SONG

Especially when dealing with limiting thoughts, such as "I'm not good enough," "I don't have enough time" or "I'll never get it done!" creating a song using a familiar tune can be fun and support release. The songs "I'm a Little Teapot," "Merrily We Roll Along" and "The Wheels on the Bus" come to mind as being especially conducive to this practice. Allow yourself to put the words in your head to the music of the song and see what happens. For bonus points, create some movement to go with it. When my client Melissa sang (to the tune of Teapot), *"I'm a little stupid on some days, can't think straight in any clever way..."* she was quickly able to recognize and release the old thought and move on with her work.

PRACTICE #24: PERMISSION TO SPACE OUT

For most people, overthinking happens. Many of us were trained to rely more on our thoughts than our emotions or sensations. But often, as Eckhart Tolle says, the mind winds up using us, rather than us using the mind.[11] Meditation is often the prescribed fix, but not everyone likes to meditate. Here's another practice to get some distance from overthinking. Give yourself permission to be spacey.

Spacing out tends to be an unconscious activity that has gotten a bad rap. It often happens when we're stressed, overwhelmed or lack sleep. But conscious spacing out can be a respite from busyness and a way to reset the system from prolonged periods of focused thinking. While spacing out can happen in stillness with eyes closed, it's also a lot of fun to move with it.

In this practice, begin by finding movement (walking works) that matches your current state of mind. Busy thinking might move quickly or frantically. And then let yourself imagine you've had a glass of wine or whatever substance you might associate with relaxing. Notice if and when your movement starts to shift. Perhaps it slows, perhaps it softens. And then do that again—take another imagined dose of your preferred relaxant and let yourself be very spacey in your movement. Can you luxuriate in not knowing what's going on? In loosening your thinking?

I had a pin many years ago that said, *"I stopped to think and forgot to start again."* And you probably don't need to worry about that, thinking tends to quickly find its way back on board.

So, for now, allow yourself to enjoy the break.

CHAPTER 5

EMOTIONS

NAVIGATING EMOTIONS

Navigating emotions can be one of life's biggest challenges. It's not taught in school, and many did not have good role models growing up. As a result, you may have learned that emotions are a sign of weakness, that they are not meant to be shared with others or that you are not allowed to feel what you do. You may have been subjected to another's outbursts and decided you would never be like that.

Emotions, whether labeled positive or negative, if not processed become toxic and show up in the physical body, informing our reactions and responses to the world and how we interact with others.

On the other end of the spectrum, we can over-identify with our feelings and allow them to run our lives. Knowing how to feel and let go of an emotion is key to navigating our daily encounters and challenges.

Emotions can be defined as energy in motion. In Chapter 3, Practice #9: Put the Feeling into Movement, I described emotions like waves on the ocean. Some feel like tidal waves, others a slight ripple on the surface. This is an easy analogy to notice in the body. That slight disturbance you felt when the restaurant was out of your favorite food may have created a tightening in your neck, face, perhaps hands. The experience of a devastating loss might be felt like a tremor in a part or the whole of your body or even a disconnection from your body completely. But whether big or small, all emotions have a beginning, a middle and an end, and will break apart and complete when allowed to fully sequence through the body and psyche.

All emotions are felt in the body. Emotions are technically just sensations we have labeled. Candace Pert, author of *Molecules of Emotion*, was the first to show emotional receptor sites throughout the body. According to Pert, our individual cells carry an electrical charge as does the body as a whole.[12] We must contact and connect with what's happening in the body to effectively let go of any emotion. **Trying to think your way out of an unwanted feeling doesn't work. And being told, or telling yourself, you shouldn't feel that way, is useless and disrespectful.**

Feelings arise and it's your job to navigate them.

SUPPRESS OR EXPRESS?

How do we navigate emotions? First, stop denying any of them. Many of us have been ridiculed or dismissed for having feelings and told a lack of emotions is strength. It's quite the opposite. Denial of feelings can be driven by people's ignorance, or lack of emotional intelligence, or out of malicious intent or wanting to be like their parents. It's a travesty that most have not been taught about emotional health as children. (One of the basic life skills missing in our education, as referenced in Chapter 2.) Instead, many have learned to suppress or hide their feelings, and many have learned to try to get rid of their feelings by yelling or blaming others. Neither way works. Suppressing can be seen as stopping short of a feeling; yelling and blaming as going past the feeling. Instead of those practices, we can learn to be present with what's happening in our bodies and stay with ourselves long enough to truly name the upset. This doesn't necessarily mean understanding why there is upset. Lesson #5 in *A Course in Miracles* says, "I'm never upset for the reason I think," which supports not trying to figure out why you feel what you do.[1] Instead, if you can be with the lump in your throat, you might recognize unvoiced anger, or the heaviness in your chest might remind you that you're not done grieving. **Different from thinking, the body informs.** With this information you can start listening to how the body wants to move through emotion. What follows in this chapter are sections on apathy; sadness and grief; fear, worry and anxiety; and anger. These are the feelings we are most likely to suppress or feel stuck in. Practices follow in each section for the specific feeling, but you might have fun experimenting with using an apathy practice for fear or an anger practice with worry. Let yourself enjoy mixing it up and breaking the rules.

You will find certain practices support the release of all emotions, including breathing, softening, opening and relaxing the body and allowing sounds to arise. Some of these practices can be found in Chapter 3. We'll be working with those concepts heavily in the practices in all the sections of this chapter.

APATHY

Apathy, though considered a feeling, is sometimes defined as a lack of feeling. It's what we experience when we don't want to do anything. Synonyms for apathy include depression, hopelessness and despair. Nothing holds any appeal, except maybe crawling into bed and pulling the blankets up. It is a heavy energy that can be challenging to move beyond. Apathy can be used as a strategy to avoid other feelings including anger and sadness. Wanting to do anything when experiencing apathy can be challenging. When in apathy, there may be resistance to letting go of apathy. An accompanying subconscious or unconscious thought may be "If I'm not apathetic, I'll have to do something." You can remind yourself that you still don't have to do anything, or that you might want to do something if you are not feeling apathetic. Asking yourself, "What can I do?" even if it's as simple as sitting up or changing your position, is something.

APATHY PRACTICES

Apathy is often accompanied by a lot of internal and external judgment. Judgment is akin to resistance, which keeps the feeling hanging around even longer. The first two practices below are about embracing the energy of apathy and are followed by practices that support slowly moving through and out of the feeling.

PRACTICE #25: BE A SLUG

The energy of apathy is heavy and slow. Embracing that energy is the first step in allowing it to be released. We might say "I feel like a slug" when in apathy. So why not move like a slug, and slither and crawl across the floor?

Technically, slugs have a band of muscle (called the central foot) that runs along the underside of their body and is covered in sticky mucus. They produce this slimy substance that creates the characteristic "goo" trail they leave behind. The mucus serves multiple purposes, including lubrication, movement and defense.

Imagine you have a central foot as your primary mode of movement. This would create a movement of elongation followed by contraction. Allow yourself to lie on your belly and imagine moving like a slug, elongating then contracting the stomach muscles to propel you, leaving behind a trail of apathy goo. You might find yourself enjoying being a slug, which will support natural progression out of apathy. A bonus to this practice is you'll be working your abdominals!

PRACTICE #26: EMBRACE SLOTH ENERGY

Similar to the slug, the sloth is known for its slow motion. Its languid, sluggish pace is something we don't often allow ourselves. The sloth travels about 41 yards a day and has the slowest metabolism of any non-hibernating land animal. Another interesting fact is that sloths move three times faster through water. This could be a two-part practice if you have access to a pool and enjoy swimming.

Part one is obvious—intentionally move slowly. If you've never seen a sloth move, find a video. Embrace the movement and feeling of being a sloth. Take three times as long to walk from the bedroom to the kitchen. Allow yourself 30 minutes to get from the car to the store. Have fun with it. Part two—get in the water. You may find that while you don't want to do anything on land, moving through water is pleasant and easy. And you've always got the option to simply float and let the water carry you.

PRACTICE #27: TAKE BABY STEPS

Apathy is an interesting energy—although we say we hate it, often, we feel pretty attached to it. It's a great hiding place, both from the self and the world. Coming out of apathy may require baby steps. So, let's start there.

A baby step may be quite literal—taking half-inch steps across the room or pretending gravity is new to you and negotiating physical balance. Or it may be less literal but still embraces the concept—like rolling over onto your stomach if you are on your back or onto your back if on your stomach. Allowing minute movements can remind your body and mind that you are capable of doing something. Movement or action doesn't need to be big for the message to be received.

PRACTICE #28: SMELL THE ROSES

Don't hurry. Don't worry. And be sure to stop and
smell the roses along the way.

Walter Hagen[13]

So much wisdom in this practice. Whether it's the roses you stopped to smell while walking to work, or the extra whiff of your morning coffee, the practice of pausing to be with what is in front of you and intentionally using the sense of smell wakes the body up. As apathy is much like putting the body and senses to sleep, this gentle act of intentionally smelling almost anything can invite aliveness.

PRACTICE #29: ALLOW SMALL MOMENTS OF JOY

Along the same lines as the earlier apathy practices, allowing yourself small moments of joy can start to support movement out of apathy. Can you blow bubbles with a straw? Play with your child's or your own toys for a minute? Even imagining walking on the beach or belly flopping into a pool could work. With these practices we are interrupting the process of misery. And once interrupted, who knows what will happen?

SADNESS AND GRIEF

You cannot protect yourself from sadness without protecting yourself from happiness.

Jonathan Safran Foer[14]

You probably don't need me to define sadness or grief for you, but many are confused about the experience of depression versus feeling sad or disappointed or bereaved. **Depression is much closer to apathy, and I think of it as a blanket covering the emotions. Sadness is only**

55

one of the many feelings we experience when grieving. Grief may also include anger, confusion, shock, denial or numbness and tends to come in waves.

Sadness can be an elusive emotion for many, and it can be hiding under anger or anxiety or fatigue, or it can be mixed in with other emotions, including joy. In the body, softening helps to reveal buried sadness.

Sadness has many flavors and, like all emotions, exists on a continuum from slight disappointment to overwhelming heartbreak. It's an emotion many are afraid to feel, believing they will get stuck in it and never function again, or fear that if they start crying, they'll never be able to stop. Many also worry about judgment or pity from others. But sadness is simply an emotion, like all others, and it too is designed to move. When we allow it, move with it, and give it permission, it can sequence and release. Many were taught their sadness was not welcome and only being happy or strong was allowed. This programming may be another obstacle to overcome.

Sadness comes with a heavy heart and is the pure emotional pain that arises with loss or disappointment. Sorrow is often repressed in favor of anger or blame, as these might feel easier to navigate or be more acceptable in society. But a feeling only moves when we accurately identify it. I've heard people say, "I've been crying for months, and the feeling is not moving." **Crying isn't always the same as being with the emotion.** Crying can happen without actually touching the true and deeper heartbreak, and one can also feel sad without crying.

Crying, when in touch with the feeling of heartbreak, rarely lasts more than a couple of minutes. And often much less than that. We can experience and move through sadness many times a day. When I'm working with clients, it's common to hear stories of abuse. As I hear these stories, my heart breaks for them. I let myself soften into the sensation so that it can move, and I can be present.

In *Way of the Peaceful Warrior*, Dan Millman says, "The heart breaks open."[15] We can use this perspective to see heartbreak as an experience that allows light in, rather than thinking sadness will break us. We can start to see the ability to feel sadness as an act of courage.

SADNESS AND GRIEF PRACTICES

As mentioned above, stepping into sadness could be a little scary. Be gentle with yourself with these practices, doing what you can when you can and backing off as necessary.

PRACTICE #30: SUPPRESSED SADNESS

If you suspect suppressed sadness in your body (and are willing to explore it), a gentle first step would be to breathe into it. Focusing especially on the exhale and letting yourself soften a little more with each breath. You may only be able to tolerate a few drops of sadness. Whatever degree of sorrow you are willing to momentarily abide is perfect. Only go to your own edge—that's where shift can happen. As you soften into sadness with your breath, you may observe sensation in your heart, your belly, your throat—sadness can be stored anywhere in the body. If you feel anything in a specific location, give that area extra breath. Notice if any images come to mind. The image can be anything—a weeping willow, a mountain stream, or yourself as a child sitting alone in a corner. Whatever comes to mind, go with it. Is there any type of movement associated with the image? If not, could you imagine how it might move? Or what might it say? This practice can be supported with writing. Use the practice of free writing, not worrying about what you write or your punctuation and spelling. What would suppressed sadness say? How do you feel about sadness? What were you taught? This practice is meant to be a gentle inquiry into what might be ready to surface and move. There is no need to rush or hurry.

PRACTICE #31: TOUCHING INTO SADNESS

If you've been uncomfortable with allowing sadness up until now, taking a gentle step in (as we did with apathy) might be wise. That might mean setting an allotted amount of time, or picking a topic, or focusing on an object that makes you feel just a little sad, to begin the practice. Allow yourself to do an internal inquiry about sadness and what it might feel like in your body. Perhaps you feel it in your throat, your heart, your stomach or someplace else. It tends to be a heavy sensation, but it also might feel like a shortness of breath or a contraction in the body. Each body is unique. Are you aware of the sadness attached to an event, a person, yourself or the world?

Whatever nudges your attention, could you sit with it without judgment? Perhaps imagine a loved one or an angel or guide sitting with you, whispering words of comfort or waiting quietly by your side. Whatever you need. The simple practice of allowing sadness to be present can go a long way, especially for those who have been taught that being sad is not allowed, is unwelcome, or scary.

PRACTICE #32: A WITCHY EXERCISE

As with everything, your experience of sadness is unique to you and what you need to move through. It may be different than what someone else needs. Honor this. And if you don't know what that is, this could be a fun practice.

Going back into history, and calling on the witch archetype, imagine you were creating a formula to cure your sadness. If we play with sadness as if it were a physical illness (which it is not, but for the sake of play...), what would cure it?

Let yourself experience the movement of throwing thoughts, feelings, memories, and whatever else wants to join, into a cauldron. Then feel yourself stirring the cauldron and even being the cauldron in response to the elements being thrown in. Whatever comes into your awareness can go into the cauldron. Whether the image or idea is an actual herb that comes to mind, or a pinch of compassion or self-pity, throw it in and move with it. This is alchemy. Notice how the ingredients shape and shift you and the sadness. You might even find yourself having fun being sad, and that's okay!

PRACTICE #33: GO AGAINST THE TIDE

As mentioned previously, the energy of sadness tends to be heavy and oppressive. We even use the words "I feel down" when referring to sadness. And it is often a pulling into self and maybe a backing up and away from others.

In this practice, allow yourself to get in touch with sadness and the natural tendency to pull in, contract, back up and go down. And then, gently shift those natural inclinations by pushing out, expanding, inching forward or moving up, while staying with the sadness. Can you even do that? What does moving forward with sadness have to teach you? Are you allowed to be in public when sad? Can you stand up for yourself and your loss, big or small? Is it allowed?

This practice can be especially useful when others tell you not to be sad. Most of the time this occurs because *they* don't know how to be with sadness. By standing up or going forward with sadness, you maintain integrity with yourself and become a role model for others.

FEAR, WORRY AND ANXIETY

Although I'm putting these three experiences together for practice, distinguishing between them will support moving with and through them.

Fear is the raw feeling we associate with imminent threat or terror. It arises quickly and is often gripping in its nature. In the moment, the sensation of fear can be felt in the chest (accompanying the holding of breath), in the stomach, or perhaps in the neck. The expression "the hair on the back of my neck stood up" comes to mind.

But we use the word fear loosely. We'll say, "I'm afraid this will happen," but in the moment we are not feeling fear; rather we're having a thought about something in the future. That type of fear is much closer to the experience of worry, which is a habit (which I address in the habits chapter). **People who worry tend to worry whether or not there's something to worry about. And, if what they're worrying about is resolved, they'll quickly find something else.** It's not a very friendly or supportive habit. Worrying never tells us about all the good that could happen, or how confident we are in handling life's challenges. Worry tells us our world is going to fall apart or is already collapsing, and we or a loved one won't be able to handle it. Worry is a particularly unpleasant companion.

We might also worry ourselves into anxiety. Anxiety is defined as excessive apprehension and could be considered anticipatory fear. Where it differs from worry is that anxiety tends to have intense sensations associated with it, like a racing heart and shortness of breath. Our thoughts, fears, and concerns about those sensations make them feel more solid and real. If anxiety had a mantra, it might be "Why postpone fear?"

Sometimes the sensations we associate with anxiety arise before we are aware of any conscious fearful thoughts or feelings. The sensations can alert us to the truth of what we are feeling. While you may be repeating positive affirmations about how strong and confident you are, your body is alerting you to fear lurking below the surface.

FEAR, WORRY AND ANXIETY PRACTICES

As uncomfortable as you may find the sensations that accompany fear, worry, and anxiety, they lend themselves well to movement.

The practices that follow will both support you in settling your body and in leaning into the sometimes bubbly sensations that arise with these experiences.

PRACTICE #34: LEARNING TO SETTLE

One of my clients has lived a life filled with anxiety. For many years, therapy, with multiple therapists, was getting her nowhere. When we started working together, we discovered she didn't know how to self-soothe. She grew up with a parent who hovered and was always there for her, to the extent that she became dependent on others to calm her down when agitated. As she discovered multiple ways to soothe herself, the anxiety settled and became an occasional experience rather than a constant companion. Settling is commonly linked to a sense of downward motion and grounding in the body. While it is true that we can settle into the ground or earth, there is much more we can or do settle into (including the couch, someone's arms and the environment you're in). In this practice we imagine settling into various energies.

Begin by picking one of the elements—earth, air, water, or fire. Which one sounds like the easiest or most fun to settle into? Let yourself imagine and/or move as if you were settling into the air. What would floating on a magic carpet feel like? Can you rest into it?

And can you settle into the ferocity of fire? Can you move frantically and still center yourself as a flame?

What about earth? Are you attracted to the pull of the planet's gravity? Afraid of it? Can you settle into or merge with the earth without wanting to go to sleep?

And the waves of the ocean? Could you be one with the current, even while it's knocking you around? If you live near the ocean, playing in the waves in all the diverse ways available can be fun and informative.

You can also settle into any part of the body. You can sink into your stomach, your hands, your feet, your heart. Does settling into your feet feel the same or different from settling into your hands or heart?

You can imagine easing into the cosmos, nestling into bed or curling up in the arms of a loved one.

Identifying as many ways as possible to "settle yourself" will give you options for different situations.

PRACTICE #35: WIND AND UNWIND

With both worry and anxiety there tends to be an experience of tightness or feeling tense, on edge. You may even use the expression "I'm all wound up." The mind has you in a spin about something or everything. **When the mind is spinning fast it can be hard to get any distance.**

Instead, actively step into the spin. Let yourself feel what your body feels like when you're wound up. Does the spin go clockwise or counterclockwise? Or is it more like the spin cycle on the washing machine and changing directions? How fast is the spin? Can you change the speed? Can you change the direction? When you change direction does the speed change? Does your breathing shift? Do you feel more relaxed or less relaxed? You can even play with this by allowing yourself to move the whole body in circles, or you can isolate it to the hands, hips or arms. Who knows what will happen when you reverse the flow.

PRACTICE #36: GIVE YOURSELF SOME SPACE

Sometimes we feel threatened by those around us or by circumstances either around us or in the wider world. Whether a real or imagined threat, the reaction in the body can be to shrink back, make ourselves small (to avoid the blow) and limit our movements. Pulling into ourselves makes the threat seem more intense. We've told ourselves through our habitual movements, "It's scary out there." Finding space for yourself can happen in diverse ways. You can physically move your body away from the threat or you can energetically and through sensation create space. Certainly, if physically moving your body away from a threat is an option, do that. If in a business meeting with a bully, plan to sit as far from them as possible.

If physically moving away is not an option, give yourself space in the body. Breathe into your belly, expand your chest and feel your feet on the ground or floor. Let yourself feel your presence (others will naturally feel strength coming from you). This would also be an appropriate time to imagine an energetic bubble around yourself. See Practice #64, Chapter 8, for a step-by-step guide to creating a bubble.

PRACTICE #37: POP THE CORK

A panic attack is often the result of trying to hold it together. Many of my clients with anxiety who have panic attacks feel like they must hold everything in, especially their feelings.

"I'm just trying to keep it together" and "I can't let myself fall apart" are common expressions for those with high anxiety.

Employ this practice when you begin to notice any internal buildup of feelings and you may avoid the more severe and uncomfortable experience of an anxiety attack.

You can imagine you are a corked champagne bottle. The idea of popping the cork for yourself may bring up more fear. But I would encourage you to try it anyway. You can always play with a smidge at a time. As they told Mikey, "Try it, you'll like it!"[16] You can always put the cork back in. Let yourself have fun mimicking the movement of the champagne after finally being released from the bottle. You can let it come out in drips or all at once. Find what feels good in your body.

If you work in a high-pressure environment, you might even want to close your office door (or use the bathroom) and do this once an hour throughout your day.

PRACTICE #38: LET YOURSELF SHAKE AND TREMBLE

When facing change, big or small, the mind can sometimes go into a fear response. We like predictability, even when we hate what's happening. When change is occurring, or is on the horizon, the mind may go into freeze mode, making you feel as if any step would be dangerous.

When you consciously allow the body to shake and tremble without resistance or judgment, you may find your mind softening, opening and seeing possibility and change in a more positive light.

Find a safe space and let yourself shake and tremble. Experiment with big and small movements as well as isolating the movement to one or two body parts and expanding the movement to the whole body. You might imagine an earthquake starting at a 1 on the Richter scale and building up to a 10. Which movement best matches what you're feeling? When you find the level that resonates and feels good, stay with it longer. Stay with it until it naturally sequences into something else or feels to you like it has moved all the way through. When the movement has completed, you will notice more internal peace and less fear.

ANGER

Anger is a tricky emotion for many of us. Messages about anger, both verbal and nonverbal, are abundant in everyone's home environment. You may have learned to hold in your anger after being told it was unattractive or being laughed at or punished for feeling it. You may have witnessed a rageaholic and confused the outbursts with being angry, and swore you'd never become that person. You may have learned to avoid conflict, either through direct teaching or from a past uncomfortable experience.

Anger exists on a continuum from irritation to rage. You may be aware of annoyance, resentment and defiance but still deny that you are angry. Reclaiming a healthy relationship with anger is critically important for everyone. **Whether we learned to suppress, or express through yelling or lashing out, both are ineffective in moving through the experience of anger.**

As with every emotion, anger can be located in sensation. It can be in the jaw, the throat, the legs, the chest or the belly. Or elsewhere. Suppressed anger has been identified as being at the root cause of many physical ailments.

But anger has a purpose—it can reveal our rights are being trampled or our boundaries have been violated, or it can be righteous indignation about atrocities in the world. Anger, when consciously owned, can propel us into action. It can support us in saying no to what and who we do not want and in saying yes to courageous action.

If we don't explore our feelings before expressing them, we increase the odds of acting from reactivity. Reactivity stems from the past. Similar scenarios we've experienced are internally awakened by the person in front of us. And reactivity begets reactivity.

It's your responsibility to process your anger before taking it to or out on another. To do the internal work of understanding what made you so angry. Was it based on current circumstances or past triggers? If based in the past, it's exclusively your work. There may have been a situation where you didn't take appropriate action, and you are actually upset with yourself. Or someone mistreated you and you were unable to protect yourself. Move through those feelings first, and then explore what, if anything, needs to happen now. If based in current circumstances, still do your inquiry first and then talk to others when necessary and appropriate. When you move through the anger first, you'll be more grounded and steadier in yourself, and your words will carry more conviction and power.

There are also circumstances where we think we're angry at another, but underneath we're really angry with ourselves. Perhaps for putting up with their behavior or for something they do that we also do. All the practices in this section also work with moving the anger one has with oneself.

ANGER PRACTICES

Anger has more energy than apathy, sadness and fear, and for many, it's easier to be with. That said, some of us were also taught to be afraid of our own anger. Again, as with previous practices, step in at your own pace. Choose one little issue and move a little anger or choose a big trigger and move a lot of anger.

PRACTICE #39: THROW A FIT

As adults, most of us have learned to keep our feelings in check (or hidden to be more accurate). In some ways, this is a good thing— we don't need to be dumping our upset onto others. But keeping our feelings to ourselves doesn't make them go away. When you acknowledge that something has seriously upset you, you might feel like throwing a fit.

Throwing a fit is good medicine! But do it for yourself and by yourself. Throw a fit intentionally and privately (or with a trusted witness/ friend) to move the feelings. Pretend you are three years old again and stomp your feet and let your arms flail. Using whatever words feel right to you, such as "This is not what I wanted," "This is not fair" or "Who do they think they are?" will support release. Once you have moved through the strong emotions, other feelings could arise.

Keep observing what's happening and allow yourself to feel what you do. Once the tidal wave subsides, you can more accurately assess if you need to take action and what that might be.

PRACTICE #40: SHAKE IT UP, DOWN, AND OFF

I love the practice of shaking with almost any feeling but find it especially powerful with anger. You may have heard or used the expression "I was trembling with rage." This is actually happening. Trembling occurs because of the body's fight or flight response, preparing the body for immediate action. When angry, your nerves are heightened, and this can cause internal or external shaking.

Trust the body's wisdom on this. Think about a person or situation you feel angry with or about. Are you aware of any shaking or trembling? If yes, go with it. Lean into the shaking, allowing it to move as it does. If not, just let your body find a rocking motion. Let it be big or small and in one part or every part of the body. You may find the rhythm of the shaking naturally shifts as you stay present with it. It may speed up, slow down, get bigger or smaller or become more rigid, more relaxed. Stay with it until it finds completion. You may uncover other feelings and experiences you've been angry about. If so, keep moving.

PRACTICE #41: DO WHAT YOU'D REALLY LIKE

Your imagination is your tool and can be amazingly helpful when you want to do all the forbidden actions. When we want to kick someone in the butt, shake the life out of them or push them over a cliff, the ability to visualize or sense doing that, can provide a wonderful outlet. And contrary to many new age teachings, letting your anger move is a step toward peace. Both internally and in the world. **Pretending you are not angry because "it's not nice or positive" is what's known as "spiritual bypass," which describes using spiritual beliefs to avoid facing unresolved emotional issues, psychological wounds, or uncomfortable realities. Instead of feigning that we are okay with everything, we let ourselves feel angry so we can get back to love.** Start by thinking about the situation that's got you upset. The more precise you can be about the anger, the more likely you will tap into what feels like appropriate retribution. If you believe you were lied to, you might want to imagine taping that person's mouth shut. If there was hypocrisy, you might want to put everything on a movie screen and show it to the world. Or you may want to hit, bite, scratch or shake them. Or destroy their most prized possessions. Whatever feels right to you. Your imagination's personal expression is not going to hurt anyone. Holding on to the anger is hurting you. In your mind's eye, go for whatever you've been fantasizing about doing to whoever or whatever stimulated your anger. If you can find the action in your body and move it, do that. Keep going until you feel a release. Allow the images to shift as they do until you find the most satisfying action.

PRACTICE #42: PUNCHING BAG

There is nothing wrong with a good old punching bag approach (or use a pillow). I've also heard that kicking a paper bag works quite well—the bag flies through the air when kicked, making some wonderful and satisfying crackling sounds. What's important in this practice is that you are intentional with your punches and kicks. Who are you punching and for what? You may need to start punching for this to be revealed. Is there something you want to say to them while you're punching them? Are there noises you want to add? Let them out!

You'll know when you're done when you can think about the people you wanted to hurt without wanting to harm them.

PRACTICE #43: LEFT WITH A BAD TASTE

Sometimes our anger with a personal situation can leave us with "a bad taste" in our mouths. It's a more subtle way of holding on to the upset, but that doesn't mean it's not affecting your body and psyche.

With this practice, we get very literal. Bring the situation into awareness and notice any sensations. The bad taste in your mouth may be joined by a sour stomach or a gagging reflex or an aching heart. Become aware of these sensations while you "spit it out." Imagine you are two years old if necessary. Note if any thoughts arise—words that may want to be spoken out loud and anything else that wants to contribute. Welcome them and express them.

PRACTICE #44: SCRIBBLE / FINGER PAINT

If you find it challenging to allow anger through the body or writing or any outlet, you might want to try this.

Choose either finger paints or a crayon, pastel, or other soft drawing instrument (allows for quick and smooth movements). Be specific with color choices and put your hand or drawing instrument to paper. Let your hand shape the movement. If thoughts arise, put them into the scribble. If no thoughts arise, go with that. Let your hand keep moving and notice if there are sensations elsewhere as you draw or paint. And keep going.

PRACTICE #45: GRUMBLE ANNOYANCE

While still on the anger continuum, annoyance is more subtle in our bodies and awareness. Sometimes annoyance is like a background hum and sometimes it's a constant nattering in our minds.

Give the grumble a voice. I have dogs to thank for this practice. Watching Kyra be annoyed with her friend during play (or with me when she's disturbed by something I did) brought the wisdom of the grumble into my awareness. Grumbling is a great substitute for complaining. Groaning and growling without words transform the emotional and mental annoyance into physical movement of the vocal cords so release can happen. Emitting expressive sounds is the opposite of what happens when we verbally complain, which keeps the issue alive and energized in our awareness. **Grumble, growl, groan, grunt, moan. Release.**

CHAPTER 6

RESISTANCE, LACK OF MOTIVATION, AND FEELING STUCK

The experiences of resistance, lack of motivation and feeling stuck are distinctly different energies with many commonalities. They all tend to lead to a lack of action and movement. And they compound each other. You may resist because you're not motivated, or say you feel stuck because you really don't want to put any effort into change. You may be feeling sluggish or drained or lacking motivation due to external factors, and then judgment and resistance show up to give that lack of motivation more strength.

Or we combine the experiences of feeling resistance and stuckness with "I don't want to, but I should," and get caught in the push-pull of what we want to do and what we think or have been told is the right thing to do.

While these topics could be included with emotions, they warrant their own discussion.

RESISTANCE

Resistance can be a powerful force for change in the world. It can just as easily be a force against the change you want in your life. Any conversation about resistance must first address the distinction.

Where conscious, intentional resistance is empowering and energy-giving, the unconscious resistance that arises for many of us day to day is just the opposite. It drains our energy and our focus and can stop us from fulfilling our dreams.

Why does resistance arise? Is it because of fear of success? Because of overworking and neglecting self-care? Is it because of a gut feeling? The answer for each desired (or sometimes necessary) change is personal and individual. Your experience of resistance is unique to you, your particular situation, and is driven by personal programming and history.

The answer to what to do about resistance is also personal. Inquiry about what drives your resistance will inform you of the answer. When engaging in the practices below, let yourself first consider what you might be trying to avoid with resistance (confrontation, confusion, physical pain or discomfort?) or what you might be trying to gain by resisting (rest, insight, help from others?).

Some years ago, my husband and I set out for a walk with Beatrice, our then 12-year-old lab mix. After going only one block, she dug her heels in, letting us know she had no interest in going any farther. I suspect Beatrice was tired from the previous day's walk and knew her body well enough not to push past her limits. Luckily, she had parents who respected her resistance. In her case, her resistance served her well. What if you had parents who didn't respect appropriate resistance? Parents who forced you to eat food you instinctively knew wasn't good for your body? How would that inform your adult relationship with resistance?

Even with conscientious and considerate parenting, resistance is common for most people.

Whether trying to change a lifelong habit, getting out of bed in the morning, or allowing feelings to arise, resistance is a familiar companion. Resistance shows up even when it comes to doing what we love. The mantra of resistance is "I don't want to." This energy can be helpful when being asked to do something that doesn't align with our values, or that we simply have no time for, but more often, resistance interferes with the goals we really want to achieve or are important to accomplish.

Resistance is defined as "energy tied up in holding, not feeling able to go with or give-in."[17] We feel it as a push-pull and become further captured by it when we blame ourselves for the resistance. It is easier to release when we recognize that resistance is an energy arising, rather than something we've consciously decided to engage in.

Resistance arises both to doing and to not doing. I don't want to clean the closet, but I also don't want the closet to be a dirty mess. And then even if I make a conscious choice not to do it, I'm still not settled. That messy closet will stay on my mind until I've cleaned it or made peace with it as it is.

Resistance can arise quickly and be a momentary annoyance or it can hang around for years, with anything, including the daily habits of brushing your teeth, drying your hair and walking the dog. It can also arise when it comes to beginning or completing a project or an unexpected opportunity. There is no shortage of material when it comes to resistance.

Resistance often arises when someone else tells us how and when and why we should do something. This is true even when it's an internal voice. That voice can be especially loud and annoying. Remember the Buddhist saying referenced in Chapter 1, "what you resist, persists"? It's true of both internal and external experiences.

When dealing with resistance, it's helpful to see it as a wave of energy arising. We may not initially identify the feeling as resistance. Instead, we blame tiredness, lack of motivation or how busy we already are. When we become aware that resistance is present, we can take a breath and let the wave of energy move through us. If we identify as being the creator of the resistance, that we are the ones who are intentionally resisting, that gives resistance more energy and strength, and we start to feel stuck in it. One of the easiest ways to work with resistance is to change your verbiage from "I'm resisting" to "resistance is arising." When you're able to do this, you've created space for the energy wave to move and dissolve.

LACK OF MOTIVATION

The lack of motivation we may feel is often connected to resistance. But lack of motivation may also exist because we don't see any reason to do whatever task is staring us in the face or quietly and persistently nagging at us, or we do not perceive a promise of fun or reward.

Lack of motivation feels quite different from resistance in the body. Think of getting out of bed in the morning—with a lack of motivation there's no reason, no energy to move, whereas with resistance it's more of a push against the world (or a pull into bed).

When experiencing a lack of motivation, it can be a result of being on the wrong path or of trying to achieve a goal that lacks intention or joy. It can also be physically driven—injury, illness and a poor diet can affect your ability to motivate yourself.

FEELING STUCK

While stuckness is associated with an inability to shift out of or change circumstances, I find "stuck" to be a word used as a catch-all for many experiences. "Stuck," similar to its relatives "stressed" and "fine," says truly little about your state of being. "Stuck" is used when there's a lack of momentum or activity in life. Or when major circumstances in your life have shifted (for example, your last child has left home). **If you catch yourself saying "I feel stuck," allow yourself to be more specific or wonder what exactly feels stuck.** Do you feel stuck between other people's opinions or desires? Do you feel stuck between two options or having no real options? Stuck in the mud? Or between a rock and a hard place? The more exact you can get with what your current experience is, the more precise you can be in moving with it and through it. (See Practice #46 in this chapter.)

When dealing with resistance and a lack of motivation, people often say they feel stuck. You may also say you feel stuck when unsure of what to do next. It can be associated with judging oneself as being too long in a feeling or situation and not knowing how to move out of it. And sometimes that feeling of stuckness or not knowing is an excuse to get out of something you know you don't want to do.

Adding movement to the feelings of resistance, lack of motivation and stuckness can support clarity and options.

RESISTANCE, LACK OF MOTIVATION AND FEELING STUCK PRACTICES

With the practices in this chapter, we embrace the energy that pairs with not wanting to or not knowing how to do something (and in embracing, dissolve the resistance to resistance). We also play with shaking up these energies so they can reveal what's below them and/ or transition into something new.

PRACTICE #46: BE STUCK

As referenced above, it can be useful to have more information about the feeling of being stuck. Think about the situation and begin an internal inquiry—What am I stuck in? What am I stuck between? What am I stuck to or with? And what's keeping me stuck?

Pay attention to the texture of what might be keeping you stuck. Is it lightweight or heavy tape, crazy glue, string or quicksand? Let yourself feel into whatever images arise. What does it feel like to be tied up or pulled down? Can you imagine being tugged in different directions? What does that movement feel like? Where in your body do you sense the bonds? On your wrists, legs, elsewhere? Play with all the different possibilities of what "feeling stuck" could translate to in your body. When you feel ready, see what unstuck might feel like. Take your time and locate these sensations or images in the body (don't just cut the tape or dissolve the glue). Feel the movements of pulling yourself out of the quicksand or softening into the rope so it naturally slackens. As the movement shifts, notice any new thoughts or feelings that might arise.

PRACTICE #47: GO SLOWER

When experiencing a lack of motivation, resistance, or feeling stuck, adopting a practice of slowing down and engaging with heightened awareness can yield valuable insights. Our society tends to move at a pace that is much too fast for most of us. And when we are moving slowly, we think something is wrong, or we're doing it wrong. When we're moving quickly, we easily bypass and miss important details. We don't hear other points of view or see options and opportunities in both our internal and external environments. Slowing down also calms the nervous system, so you get a natural release. **Allowing slowness to be welcome in your day-today activities will help regulate your nervous system, let you become more aware of your feelings and environment and quite likely will help you do what you want to get done more efficiently.**

As you slow down, ask yourself "What's the hurry?" or "What's here right now?" or "What am I seeing, feeling, hearing, sensing?" Slowing down also reduces cortisol (stress hormone), enhances focus and concentration, improves productivity and allows for creativity. And often, when we allow ourselves to go slower, resistance dissolves, motivation arises and stuckness finds movement. Trying to go at a pace that is too fast for you may be at the root of these experiences.

You might not be resistant to going or doing, but simply to going or doing too quickly.

Walking to the mailbox in twice the time it usually takes, or driving the speed limit (rather than 5, 10 or 15 mph faster) and pausing to smell the roses as you're on a walk are all ways to practice slowing down. It may be uncomfortable—when you slow down, you're more likely to become aware of what you're feeling; you may remember pressure from others to hurry (whether or not there's anything that requires hurrying); you may feel guilty for taking a moment to yourself. Or you may love it. You may feel like you can finally hear yourself think, be present with yourself and enjoy the little things. Remember that it's all an inquiry.

Practices #25 and #26 in Chapter 5 on moving with apathy embrace the slow movements of the slug and the sloth and may be worth revisiting.

PRACTICE #48: GO FASTER

In general, I don't advocate going faster. But there is wisdom in all things. If you find yourself feeling sluggish, stuck, unmotivated or down in general, speeding up might be exactly the medicine you need.

Going out for a quick run will literally get your body moving. Or walk across the room twice as fast as your usual pace. Simply putting your body into another gear can invite action. Another benefit of going fast is not having the time to overthink. And if you're an overthinker, you know that too often we use empty time to mess with ourselves. Speeding up and having less time to review and consider and wonder about all the options often works in our favor. Unlike in the slowing-down process, I don't recommend this practice while operating heavy machinery.

You could also use windup toys to get in touch with the energy of going fast. On the TV game show, *The Price is Right*, one of the games is betting on which color windup rat will reach the finish line first. You might imagine being the fastest rat, then the slowest rat, and see what you notice.

PRACTICE #49: WALK TOWARD IT

This practice of letting go can be helpful when you've been wanting something for a long time without making progress toward achieving or having it.

Maybe you've been longing for a new job, a new relationship or even recognition from your boss. While there's nothing wrong with an occasional enjoyable fantasy, when we live in longing (without action), it winds up reinforcing a sense of lack or the feeling of being stuck. Long-term desire often comes with fantasies about how life would change if this or that happened and/or self-beliefs explaining why it will never happen. Putting your body into motion may reveal added information.

Start walking (or imagine walking) in the direction of what you want. Feelings may start to arise. You may find excitement and/or fear. Perhaps there's a fear of being laughed at, a fear of not deserving or not being good enough. You may even find as you walk toward the object of your desire that you're not as interested in having it as you thought. And what you really want is the fantasy of having it. Knowing this would allow you to release the angst about not having it and allow you to enjoy imagining.

If, on the other hand, you've encountered fear in some form, that's the next thing to explore and let go of.

PRACTICE #50: DO SOMETHING, ANYTHING AT ALL

This is a great practice for your "stuck on the couch" self, when it feels like doing anything is too much.

When feeling a lack of motivation, even practices designed to help you find motivation can be met with resistance and be accompanied by thoughts such as "I don't have enough energy," or "That's going to take too long" or "Why won't someone else do it?"

Employing a practice of wondering about what you **can** do might produce different outcomes. Here's the simple practice—in those moments where you don't feel capable of doing what you think you should be doing, simply ask, "What can I do?" Can you roll over onto your stomach? Can you sit up instead of lying down? Can you touch your toes or your knees? Even a little movement will invite more movement. Continue the process with the next possibility. Can I walk to the mailbox? Write myself a note about all the things I'm thinking about and avoiding right now? Take a shower? Have a cup of tea? Simply getting the body in motion can be an incentive for more action.

You may notice this practice is similar to some of the practices we used for apathy and wonder which came first—the feeling or the behavior?

PRACTICE #51: CHUNK IT DOWN

When facing a large project that seems daunting, thoughts like "It's too much," "I'll never get it done," etc., can add to a lack of motivation.

Committing to taking small steps such as spending 15 minutes on your project or writing two paragraphs or folding five items of clothing may help you start.

To put this concept into movement, let yourself walk across the room taking tiny steps (or even crawling). Eventually, if you keep going, you'll make it to the other side of the room. While this might seem silly, this practice will remind you that even little steps can propel you in the direction of what you want.

PRACTICE #52: SWIVEL

This is a fun one! You'll need a swivel chair for it. At work or at home (or at home working) if you catch yourself feeling low energy, resistant or stuck in your mind about your next steps, pause whatever you're doing and let yourself swivel in both directions in your chair. If you hold onto your desk or a counter while doing this, you can increase the speed. There's an added benefit of a little workout! Let yourself have fun playing with tempo and how far you swivel. You could even start with the smallest amount of movement that matches your current state of mind. Notice what happens if you go way faster or bigger or play with small increments. **Try it now and feel the energy shift!**

And if you don't have a swivel chair, swivel your upper body in a stationary chair or stand up and swivel or twirl on your feet.

PRACTICE #53: PRACTICE NOT KNOWING

Feeling stuck at a job, in a relationship or in a living situation because of not knowing what else you would do or what will come next if you leave is not unusual. **The mind hates not knowing. The body, on the other hand, is fine moving without knowing what it's doing.**

Allow yourself to play with the positions typically associated with not knowing. Shoulders lifted, palms open, eyes up are common ones. Put on some music (maybe even a child's tune) that allows you to move around without any particular purpose or direction. Let yourself be silly and have some fun. You might even add some galumphing (moving in a clumsy, noisy, inelegant manner) to your play.

This practice will remind your cellular system and your brain that you're not going to die if you don't know what's going to happen.

PRACTICE #54: STATUE COMING TO LIFE

This practice, inspired by the moving statues in Las Vegas and other tourist destinations, can be used when feeling stuck or unmotivated. You can imagine yourself as a statue made from marble, clay, sticks or metal (like the Tin Man in Wizard of Oz). Each will feel slightly different. And the practice is much as it sounds. Allow yourself to assume the unmoving statue position. Choose a starting position that represents your current mood. Maybe your head is in your hands or on the desk, you're standing in a slumped-over position, or your arm is stuck in midair like the Tin Man. What best demonstrates your feeling of stuckness or lack of motivation?

Then, bit by bit, allow your body to come to life. You can imagine your elbow being oiled, or your shoulders massaged into movement. You might start with a very slight tilt of the head, or the fingers might start to open, or the jaw might relax and soften. You can let each part of the body have its turn, or they can all slowly come to life simultaneously. Adding appropriate sounds such as squeaks and moans can enhance the experience. The more fun you have with being stuck and getting unstuck or feeling movement, the better. You are effectively taking resistance out of the formula. Maybe you even need to melt like the Wicked Witch of the West.

PRACTICE #55: REVISIT THE SKELETON AND THE JOINTS

In Chapter 3, Practice #11, we explored joints and how they impact your ability to change course, and in Practice #12, we played with going loosey-goosey like a skeleton to find relaxation in the body. In this practice, we bring those two together, moving as a skeleton and relying on the joints.

If a skeleton were able to move on its own, it would have to rely on the joints. The joints are about direction and give us movement options. Without elbows the arms would not bend, without wrists writing would be challenging and without hips and knees you won't get far from your current position.

Allow yourself to imagine you are all bones and joints and need to get from here to there (anywhere will do). With no muscles to propel you, moving even an inch will require some joint action. You might find yourself bending, twisting and falling, or using arm bones and joints to move leg bones. Exploring alternative ways to propel the body can open the mind to alternative ways of doing.

CHAPTER 7
PESKY HABITS

Many of our finely-tuned, often-used habits do not support health and well-being. In fact, they often support feeling stressed and a sense of lack.

WORRYING

Starting with the **worry habit**, it's important to note worrying is a learned behavior. If you consider yourself a worrier, it's likely you have had worrying demonstrated by one of your primary caregivers. The good news is that learned behaviors can be unlearned with practice. **Worry is a fear-based behavior and supports the belief that the world is a scary place and affirms the belief that you are not capable of handling what happens.**

Fear is an emotion with accompanying sensations that we can feel, validate, process and release. Worry, on the other hand, is a practice of distressing yourself. According to the Merriam-Webster Dictionary, "worry" means "to afflict with mental distress or agitation: make anxious." Worry is saying to yourself consciously or unconsciously, "Bad stuff is coming, and you better be scared." As if being scared will prepare you for what's coming. Wouldn't it be kinder and more self-affirming to tell yourself that you are capable and competent in facing life's challenges?

Many believe their worry habit is ingrained, and they will never be free of the hard-wired worrying. Recognizing that worry is a habit and not a feeling can help you transform your relationship with it. It requires commitment and intention, but breaking a habit is doable.

Wondering, "What do I gain from worrying and what would happen if I were free from worry?" is a good first inquiry.

You may think you'll forget what you want to get done if you don't worry. That's an easy fix— write yourself a note or set an alarm. Much easier on the system.

You might think if you let go of worrying, you won't be prepared to handle a person or situation. But worrying puts you and your body in a contracted state which is not a condition in which you can easily assess your strengths.

Someone you know and love may be ill, and you're worrying about them. Rather than worrying, consider asking yourself and them what might be helpful for their well-being. Also take the time to check in with yourself. Are you feeling hopeless, concerned about not being able to handle the grief, guilty about something you did or didn't do? You may uncover multiple feelings under the surface.

PROCRASTINATION

Procrastination is the habit of postponement. Most of us are very familiar with putting off doing what we dislike and also putting off doing what might bring up feelings we don't like. Whether it's the dishes or telling a friend you can't make the movie, there's an internal "uck" and a feeling of wanting to avoid something, which drives procrastination. A big issue with procrastination is its persistent nature. When we neglect a responsibility, task, or chore, there is a lingering internal dialogue perpetually haunting us with reminders that we "should be doing it." This ongoing internal conflict tends to increase resistance and further perpetuate procrastination. Whenever anyone tells us to do something, including or especially ourselves, there's that knee-jerk reaction of "you can't make me."

Moving out of the energy of procrastination can be challenging because of this push-pull with ourselves. Engaging playfully with the parts of yourself that try to push you into doing and the parts that push back can be one way to loosen the grip of the push-pull. Finding enthusiasm or building motivation into the task can also be supportive. Add music to housecleaning, write at the coffee shop or think about the next task while walking the dog. When we add enjoyment to a task it becomes considerably more palatable. As Mary Poppins taught us: "A spoonful of sugar helps the medicine go down!"[18]

WANTING

Wanting things and experiences is another path we take that turns a feeling into a habit. Instead of noticing when the feeling of desire arises (and moving with the feeling), we become fixated on having certain things and it can become all we think about. We not only want money, vacations, health, love and fun, we also want the world and other people to be different than the way they are. And we think we'll be satisfied or happy when we get what we want. Have you ever stopped to consider all you currently have that you once wanted? Did it fix everything? Probably not. It's possible you've seen some shift. If you wanted someone to help with your busy life and you hired an assistant, your life may be easier. But often, we strive to have more money in the bank or to lose weight thinking it will make us happy. And when it doesn't, we move on to wanting what's next on the list that "will make everything okay."

I remember being in a jewelry store many years ago and noticing I wanted many more items than I had planned on purchasing. I was able to identify the feeling of lust in the moment. I stood in the store and let myself become aware of the feelings and sensations that accompanied lust. I asked myself questions like "What do you think that will do for you?" and "What's it going to feel like if you have it or don't have it?" Exploring my feelings loosened their grip. I was able to purchase the necklace and earrings I intended to buy, and left feeling satisfied rather than disappointed that I couldn't have more.

Wanting anything affirms a sense of lack. Would you want it if you already had it? Living with "I have enough or plenty" versus "I need more" is a very different experience. When you can acknowledge and appreciate what you already have, that gratitude attracts more. It's part of the human experience to desire, but the more we can let go of any feelings or attitudes that we "must have" something, or that it will not be okay if we don't have something, then the more ease we feel in our lives. When we are more at ease, life seems to happen effortlessly, and we are more apt to take action.

PESKY HABITS PRACTICES

Moving through habits is a little different than moving through thoughts and feelings. You might think of habits as a shell encasing thoughts, feelings and past experiences. The term "breaking habits" can be interpreted as the need to crack the shell and see what lies within. If you find yourself encountering stuck or negative thoughts, you may want to revisit Chapter 4. If feelings are uncovered, remember what we worked with in Chapter 5.

PRACTICE #56: EMBRACE PLAY—WITH CHARACTERS

In Chapter 2, we looked at how play can support letting go. It is another highly underrated therapeutic tool. Especially for breaking habits. Many of our habits originated in play— mimicking or trying on what our parents or others role-modeled. You may recognize that you worry like your mom or chase money (or women) like your grandpa or put yourself low on your priority list (yes, not meeting your needs is also a habit) based on what was exemplified in your home. Playing with the parts of you (as if they were separate characters) that engage in these habits can be very revealing.

In this practice, think of one habit that may not be in your best interest. And then, give that part of you a name. Maybe it's simply the worrier, the procrastinator or the luster. But maybe a name pops into your mind (don't be surprised if it's someone from your past). Give that character full control for a minute or two. What do they say? How do they move? Do they gesture? What are their facial expressions? Once you have a good sense of this character's qualities, start playing with them. Make them bigger, smaller, louder, quieter. Soften or tighten the movements, speed them up or slow them down. Keep going until you're amused. If you find yourself laughing at yourself, even better. **Laughter is a natural dissolver of held patterns.**

PRACTICE #57: INVOKE DR. SEUSS

The benefits of rhyming for improving language skills, memory and writing are well documented. Rhyming also supports the expansion of imagination and induces joy. The pleasure rhyming brings to a child when first learning a language is immense and often results in extended giggling episodes. When we take our worries (or procrastination or wanting) into rhythmic patterns, we are stepping into play and imagination, a wonderful place to let go from.

This practice doesn't need much explanation. Think about one of your current concerns, and whatever comes to mind, put it to rhyme. Here's a silly sample to get you started:

The sky is falling
I'll be crawling
On my knees
Through the weeds.
It won't get done,
There will be no fun
And I'll have no time to hang with my hun.

Don't worry about producing a good work of art. Your rhyme is for you. For bonus points, make up a dance (even a hand dance) you could teach a five-year-old with your rhyming words. I'm reminded of "The Itsy Bitsy Spider" and the hand gestures of going up the waterspout.

PRACTICE #58: SPIN THE PLATES

This practice is especially good for when you're feeling overwhelmed, like "there's too much on my plate" or that you'll never get it all done. And while you could attempt this practice with real poles and plates, using your imagination will work quite well.

First, allow yourself to consider all the responsibilities you're managing in your mind. Get an approximate count (10, 20, 50, 100, thousands?) and then imagine having a porcelain plate balancing on a pole for each appointment, chore, duty, task, person and event that you're managing. Then, like the circus performers, try to keep them all spinning. This is a great time to physically add the motion of your hands spinning the imaginary poles. Have fun spinning them for as long as you do, and when you're ready, let them all crash to the floor. Rejoice in the imagined sounds and mess you'll make. And notice, with everything crashing around you, you are still standing. And feeling a bit lighter! Now walk away; you don't have to clean up an imagined mess!

PRACTICE #59: ON DUTY / OFF DUTY

Sometimes the habit of worrying feels so ingrained it may seem like there's no off switch and you're on duty all the time, even when sleeping. This practice will help remind you worry is not akin to breathing and, in fact, you won't die if you take a break.

In this practice, let yourself imagine you're one of the guards at Buckingham Palace on high alert. Feel the posture, the steps, the arm movements and the facial expressions as you become the guard. Stay with it long enough to identify the level of tightness and tension in your body. On a scale of 1 to 10 (10 being super tight and closed in), how tight are you?

Then, imagine it's the changing of the guards and you're going off duty. What does that transition look like or feel like? Is it a fast or slow process? Can you fully go off duty or do you stay at some level of alertness?

This practice may bring up thoughts and feelings from the past or present about being on alert. Be with these experiences to whatever degree you're able, breathing with them. If necessary, write them down to process at a later time.

PRACTICE #60: PLAY WITH ANYTHING

Play with the dog, the kids, the cat, or a windup toy. It doesn't matter what type of play you engage in as long as you fully engage. In Practice #56, we played with characters as a way to tap into and release what was formed while imitating others in childhood. In this practice, we tap into the transformational qualities of play for its own sake. We took a first step into random play with Practice #5. Play brings us into the current moment and allows for new direction. Play brings us to a choice point, where we can decide to return to the thinking, feeling and actions we had been engaged with, or we can choose a different path. Especially helpful if you find yourself procrastinating, feeling lazy or resistant.

Allow yourself to play tug-of-war with the dog (you could even imagine the tug between the parts of yourself that want to and don't want to), roll on the floor by yourself or with the kids, build a tower from objects on your desk and knock it down or take a dance break. Step away from the phone and all electronic devices. Walk around the block and look for the rainbow colors in nature. Stop at the playground and let yourself swing or climb on the monkey bars. Your body knows how to play. Let it.

PRACTICE #61: TAKE A SOUND BATH

Sometimes, we need soothing more than anything else. The nervous system is on high alert (or low—procrastination could be an attempt to regulate the system) and needs help settling.

You can move with this practice or just sit and feel the sounds moving through you. This practice can be done with calming music of your choice or the sounds of nature. Allow the sounds to move from head to toe through your body. Play with broad sweeps of sound—like ocean waves moving through you, as well as drips or drops at a time, or like a waterfall or a shower you can regulate. Let the sound reach into the crevices of your body and every single cell. Luxuriate for as long as you can.

PRACTICE #62: REACH AND YIELD

Wanting anything or anyone can easily be seen as reaching for something outside ourselves. As so many in the spiritual, psychological, and self-help realms have taught for a very long time, what we most want does not come from outside of ourselves. The source is inward and so is the journey.

Feeling the reach of wanting in the body can happen through the arms, eyes, hands, fingertips (the endpoints), and can also be felt in the heart, stomach or other areas of the body.

Let yourself think about something you want. And go ahead and reach for it in any way that feels right. And as you're reaching, maybe you want to crawl toward it or feel pulled to it. Have fun with the movement and experience of wanting, reaching and crawling. You may even want to exaggerate the movements and see if you notice something different.

Maybe you're reminded of how long you've been reaching and not getting what you want.

When you feel ready, let go of the reach and soften your shoulders, breathe into your belly, and feel your feet in contact with the ground. Then allow yourself to find a yield in the body. Opening, allowing and softening into yourself. Yielding is not giving up but finding a relaxed place from which to engage. Feel what's different in this position. Perhaps a new thought about what you've been wanting comes to mind. New avenues can open. Or you can recognize you're just fine whether or not you acquire the object or person or experience you desire.

CHAPTER 8

RELATIONSHIPS

RELATING

For most of us, the word "relationship" immediately brings to mind the people we are in a significant relationship with or the people we wish to be in a relationship with. We also "relate to" co-workers, neighbors, friends and the people in line at the market. But relating to others is only one aspect of the relating we do daily. We also relate to the ground, the weather, the furniture, and of course, our breath and our bodies. Before we ever start engaging with another, we're aware of the ache in our back, the chill in the air, the urgency to use the bathroom. In Chapter 3, we began the exploration of learning to listen to our bodies. We revisit it here in the context of healthy relationships.

Being aware of what's present in our physical body, in the emotional system and our energy field—in other words, listening to and respecting ourselves—is the most important relationship we will ever have. **And only when we have a healthy relationship with ourselves are we able to create healthy relationships with others.** Healthy relationships can only happen between two healthy people.

Being aware of how you relate to the wind and the rain, itchy materials, loud sounds and other things you encounter daily, enables you to engage in more refined self-care. And when you take diligent care of yourself, it's much easier to take loving care of others. Knowing how much people-time you can tolerate, how often you want to be with someone else (this will differ by person) and how close or far you need them to be for you to feel safe and loving, will support your ability to set appropriate limits and boundaries in your relationships.

BOUNDARIES

Some of us have one person in the world we can imagine spending day in, day out with for more than three days. More often, we can love people better with more distance between us or less time engaged with them. That distance may come in the form of miles away, time spent or what you choose to share. It's up to you to determine what this distance is with relatives, friends and anyone in your circle of regular contact.

Healthy relationships are built on mutual respect and include healthy boundaries. From Dr. David Gruder: "A boundary is any limit I need to honor so I can love or work with you without resentment and with integrity."[19]

Healthy relationships are dependent on healthy, respected boundaries.

Boundaries are a critical aspect of self-care and are also about taking care of the relationship. Once we've established how much time or energy we want to put into any relationship, it becomes our job to communicate that to others. The way we let others know how close we want them to be, physically or emotionally, is through our boundaries.

With respectful, aware people, we may not need to set boundaries. They are already tuned in to our energy and have the emotional intelligence to know when to keep their distance. Not everyone is sensitive. Sometimes people violate our boundaries thinking they are helping or taking care of us. And while it's true that the person reaching out may be extending from sincere motivation, it's still a boundary violation. Overbearing and interfering parents or caregivers may have violated our boundaries repeatedly, diminishing our ability to even know what our boundaries are. This could be accompanied by a belief that we are not allowed boundaries, or we are not permitted to have boundaries with certain people. It's challenging to find a sense of self when others are always doing for us and telling us what to do, including telling us what to feel.

You set boundaries verbally, energetically and physically. And you set limits differently with different people and in different environments. Sitting alone in a coffee shop, if you don't want to be disturbed, you may avoid eye contact, shift the angle of your body, or move to a different table to let others know you don't want to engage.

When on the phone or even a video call, it might be more important to use words. Communicating that you're done with a topic, or the phone call itself, may require you saying aloud in a kind, but firm way, "I'm done."

And what about respecting another's boundaries? How are we supposed to know when they don't want to engage or be touched? Or texted 90 times a day? The answer is simple. Pay attention! What are they communicating through their bodies and actions? Did they tell you they don't have time to text at work? Are they always rushing to get off the phone or interrupting or cutting you off? They may not be willing to say it's too much, but they are showing you with their responses or lack thereof. And though it's not your job to read nonverbal clues, doing so can definitely make your life easier and your relationships more enjoyable. And it may be time for you to let go of some of your expectations and demands.

If you've unintentionally violated a boundary, no big deal, apologize. But how do you know if you are unintentionally and regularly violating others' boundaries?

Make a habit of self-inquiry. Do you always feel a little off after an interaction with someone? Besides the signals the other may be trying to send you, your body is likely sending signals as well.

Same if someone continues to violate your boundaries. Do you need to get louder or possibly end the relationship? All relationships should be mutually respectful, even those with your family members. Expectations can be boundary violations. The relative who expects you to drop everything if they need you, the co-workers who expect you'll clean up their mistakes, and the clients who rely on you to text when they've forgotten an appointment with you. Their expectations are reinforced by your silent compliance. You are allowed to say what you want or require in the relationship. You won't always receive the consideration you ask for, but that's just more information for you about the other. And then you decide how to move forward.

It's important to know and remember that not all relationships should be salvaged. It takes two healthy people to engage in healthy relating. There are times when leaving or letting a relationship go is absolutely the most appropriate action.

This chapter and the practices in it are devoted to your relationships with yourself and others. And I understand if you feel the desire to skip over the relationship with yourself, the internal work takes courage. Engaging in self-reflection is not for the weak. It's a lot easier to blame others, to look to someone else to feel a sense of connection or to lean into the ego's defaulting principle, "everything is about me." But as you contact what's authentically you, your relationships with others can only become healthier and more satisfying.

RELATIONSHIP PRACTICES

PRACTICE #63: FORGIVENESS

Holding on to resentment is never a good thing. It creates havoc in your body and can occupy your mind and drain your energy. It destroys relationships as fast as anything. Often, the resentment is toward oneself for tolerating certain behaviors. As you're doing this practice on resentment toward others, also check if there's any toward yourself. In Chapter 5, we worked with many practices to let go of anger and resentment. Go there first if necessary.

Forgiveness in the body might be described as emptiness. It's a release of what's been held and does not need to be replaced with love or light or any other thought or feeling.

Allow yourself to notice where you feel an old resentment held in the body. It could be in the heart, the belly, the neck or the toes. And then, could you imagine emptying that area? You might take a conscious breath in, and on the exhale, feel yourself emptying. If it needs sound or movement, go for it. If something feels stuck, visit the practices on stuckness in Chapter 6. If there's more anger, go back to emotions in Chapter 5. See if you can reach empty. And then check if empty feels good or uncomfortable. Can you be with whatever else arises? Or is there more? And if there is more, do you need to give yourself a boundary of how much you can work on in any given practice and plan to come back to it when ready?

PRACTICE #64: ENERGY BUBBLE

When in the presence of others, it's easy to lose track of ourselves. **We forfeit awareness of self in favor of awareness of others and their needs.** Besides the very obvious issue of being oblivious to our own needs, it also results in the experience of not fully showing up for others. When their needs become our primary focus, we forget who we are and that we need to bring ourselves to the relationship. The other person may feel like they don't know where their friend or partner went, even when sitting in close proximity.

An energy bubble helps us feel the energy from within that surrounds us. It's a protective shield emanating from deep within us. There are many ways to create your shield using artwork, music, and imagination. I was taught, and teach others, to create an energy bubble by first connecting to each of the seven primary energy centers in the body (the chakras). Starting with the base chakra (at the base of the spine), then moving to the sacral chakra (below the belly button), the solar plexus (abdomen/above the belly button), the heart, the throat, the third eye and up to the crown of the head. Pause at each chakra and breathe into the area and imagine each center opening like a blossom. You can add the corresponding colors: red, orange, yellow, green, blue, indigo and violet (listed in order from base to crown). And then, feel the flow of energy spiraling up and down the energy centers like the spin on a barbershop pole. See that pole as a tube of energy and allow it to expand into a bubble shape and a size that's comfortable for you. Play with the color of your bubble. It may be clear and white when alone, but around others you prefer a deeper color that feels less permeable. If there are highly problematic people in your environment, you might want to arm your bubble with a protective shield or daggers. Whatever it takes in your imagination for you to feel safe and protected in your energy and space.

Once you have your bubble, let yourself move through space feeling the awareness of your bubble. If your bubble expands five feet around you, and someone stands two feet away from you, what are the internal experiences? Maybe you even start to notice someone else's energy bubble!

PRACTICE #65: BE A PUPPET

Sometimes, in relationships, we feel as if the other person is controlling us. Sometimes, we feel like we're trying hard to control ourselves. Either way, the feeling of being controlled is not fun. Unless we make it so.

In this practice, imagine you are the puppet with strings attached in as many areas of the body as you can think of. And then let yourself be pulled, twisted and manipulated in all the ways you experience those sensations. As you keep moving, you may find yourself pulled into a dance. It's important you allow yourself to enjoy feeling controlled as much as you can. This might come as a surprise, but when someone else is in control, we might feel like we don't have to be. And then, instead of resisting it, we can enjoy it. As you continue to embrace the joy of being controlled, it might start to shift. You might find you don't like all those strings after all. What would your movement look like if you cut the strings? This might take some exploration. Allow it to go in whatever direction it does.

PRACTICE #66: PAT YOURSELF ON YOUR BACK

One of the common relationship dynamics is looking for recognition, love and approval from others. We seek outside of ourselves to access love instead of tapping into the love that is our essence, the energy that is always present even when we are unaware of it.

Lesson #197 in A Course in Miracles is "It can be my gratitude I earn."[1] Learning to appreciate ourselves and what we can give, what we are capable of and who we are, is literally a gift that keeps on giving. It fills the body from the well of love that is innate.

Practicing physical acknowledgement of yourself jumpstarts recognition, appreciation and self-love. Pat yourself on the back, tell yourself all the wonderful things you did today, write them down and give yourself a gold star for each. Talk to yourself like you are your favorite person in the world.

PRACTICE #67: PUT THE RELATIONSHIP INTO MOVEMENT

When caught in a relationship dynamic that's not working, it's fun to imagine and actually put into movement the dance that's currently happening. Perhaps it feels like one partner is a strong leader, while the other follows well (or not so well), or maybe it's more like a tug-of-war type dance without a lot of rhythm or flow. And maybe the music you're dancing to is hard rock or something that grates on your nerves.

In your mind's eye, or for real, change the music and dance a different dance. What would it feel like to do a fun cha-cha or a smooth waltz? Maybe you want to play with a dangerous paso doble or a sexy rumba or a tango? Whether you know the name of the dance or not, check if the dynamic feels fluid, sharp, fast, slow, rigid, and let yourself wonder how that impacts you. As you contrast the current qualities with the opposite (slowing down or speeding up, softening, getting more directive), how does that change how you feel and interact with the other? If you change the music to something more upbeat, what happens? What if you danced side-by-side rather than face-to-face? Let yourself keep playing with different options and notice the changes in your body and potential changes in the relationship dynamic.

When one person shifts how they engage in the relationship, the other will often shift in response without even realizing it.

PRACTICE #68: WALK AWAY

Sometimes you may feel caught in a situation or a relationship that doesn't feel right. It's possible you've been complaining about it for years but still haven't literally walked away. When immersed, it can be hard to have perspective. Experimenting on your own with the practice of walking away can support or inform what you do with others.

Allow yourself to take a step back to start. Perhaps you even want to pretend you're watching a movie with yourself as the lead character while you are physically moving. Draw a picture of the relationship if you think it would be helpful. When you step back, what do you see and become aware of? How does the dynamic look when you are not entangled in it? What do you learn about yourself or others from watching?

As best you can, watch without judgment. The critical mind clouds your vision, and you see only what you've always seen. Without judgment, you can see options that will make the situation more comfortable or the relationship more enjoyable. Or you might see it really is time to walk away.

PRACTICE #69: PLAYING ROLES

You play many roles in your lifetime and your day-to-day activities. Sometimes you're the teacher, sometimes the student. You may be the driver or the passenger (literally or figuratively), the one who knows everything, or the one who pretends not to care about anything. You may play the role of someone who doubts themselves or you may play the role of the authority figure, the obedient one or the troublemaker. Maybe you're the one who incites trouble or action in your family, but acts the subservient employee at work.

Sometimes these behaviors become so familiar you think you are the role you're playing. Then you are trapped and limited and unable to show up in all the many diverse dimensions of who you actually are. One day you may not want to be the caretaker; you may want to be the careless one. Playing with these behaviors as separate internal characters can help you recognize you have options in navigating them and can use them as strategies or let them go, depending on circumstances.

Think of one of the roles you frequently play and imagine turning that part of you into a television or movie character. How would that character dress? Move? Sound? Let yourself take on the characteristics and exaggerate and contrast them. If the tendency is to be soft-spoken, start there and gradually become even softer and then grow much louder. See what happens.

If you're always playing the role of leader, you might start by marching around imagining many followers and then shift to being a follower. You could even play with this at the supermarket (just don't stalk anyone).

If you're the one who never speaks up in a group, try saying something. If you're always the one who speaks up, experiment with not saying anything. Almost any behavior can be played with as a role. And as you become more familiar with the roles you play in your primary relationships, you may find you're ready to switch it up.

PRACTICE #70: TURN DOWN THE VOLUME

For many, the world and the sounds coming from others are too loud. The constant noise of traffic, voices, electronics, construction, and life itself can be overwhelming. Physically and internally contracting to defend against the noise is natural. There may even be sounds you think you've tuned out (like the refrigerator or the dishwasher) that are having an impact on your body. Bringing awareness to the sounds you're hearing and any tightening in your body allows you to soften and open (Chapter 3, Practice #14) and give the sound space. Simply see what happens as you let the sounds be, without resisting them. Experiment with matching the sound. Many dogs do this in response to sirens—it naturally makes the sound easier to tolerate and helps their nervous system to settle.

You might also pay attention to how you react to loud voices—do you get louder or shut down? Maybe you walk away? Do you get softer, hoping others will follow your lead? This is a practice you might want to bring into your awareness intentionally for a week or two. Notice your reactive response to sound as you move through the world. And let yourself experiment with different responses.

PRACTICE #71: CHANGE YOUR BODY LANGUAGE

We interact with others at least as much through body language as we do with verbal language. According to Albert Mehrabian's 7-38-55 model, only 7% of a message comes from words, 38% from tone, and 55% from body language.[20] Other studies confirm this saying that significantly more of our communication is nonverbal than verbal.

Much of our conversation is unconscious or subconscious. The hands, face, pelvic floor and feet are the endpoints through which we communicate most directly. We also communicate through movement and gesture, as in turning our backs on someone.

Are you aware of the ways in which you use your eyes, hands, pelvis, feet and movements to communicate in relationships? Notice if you reach for others or push them away as a general rule. Notice if you shrink back into yourself when in the presence of others to avoid attention. Or do you get louder and bigger, to make sure no one misses you? How often do you avert your eyes (or turn the other way) to avoid engaging with someone? Observing your nonverbal expression is another facet of this practice you could take with you for a week or two. Notice your habitual body language as well in response to others and see if you like those responses or if you prefer another way of engaging. Be aware of what happens in your conversations when you change your body language. If you stop keeping your arms crossed against your chest, is anyone nicer to you? Or does that make them move away from you? Or something else? Take note if people pay less or more attention if you open your eyes wide or sit up straight. Recognizing all the modes you currently use to communicate through your body, take note of what works for or against you and your relationships. You have immense power to shift your relationships by playing with and having fun changing your styles of body language.

PRACTICE #72: HAVE WHAT YOU WANT

In any ongoing relationship with another, you desire certain things from them. Maybe you want them to demonstrate more physical or emotional support, maybe you want them to listen better, keep their promises, and acknowledge all that you do. What we want from others can be based on something we did not get enough of in childhood or something we are not good at giving to ourselves (being listened to, acknowledged, supported, time alone). Yes, as a child, your parents are supposed to meet your needs (at least in most societies), but as an adult, expecting others to meet your needs is often a setup for relationship failure. When you learn to meet your own emotional needs, it changes your expectations and allows for more love in your relationships.

For this practice, think about something you've been wanting from others. It may be tied to an internal mantra, such as "no one ever listens to me" or "I feel like I never get any acknowledgment or support." Once you identify what you want from others, find ways to give those things to yourself. Give yourself a hug, a pat on the back, some words of recognition. Go crazy and find some pom-poms and do cheers for yourself. You deserve to be celebrated and to have your needs met and you don't need someone else to do that for you. If and when they do, it will be icing on the cake.

CHAPTER 9
GOALS AND FREEDOM

GOALS AS A GATEWAY

Call it a goal or not, we all want more of some things and less of others. **Desire comes with being human. And often desire comes with suffering.** In our minds, we turn our wanting into needs and our goals into something we must attain to prove ourselves. There is no freedom in this. But goals can serve a purpose on the path to feeling free. Lester Levenson, originator of the Sedona Method®, taught goal setting as a method to identify limiting beliefs and minimize the suffering that can accompany longing and lack.[4]

The exploration includes getting curious about the motivation behind having a particular goal and what may be blocking the attainment of that goal. I love this approach to working with goals. In it is permission to set goals out of curiosity and interest. To wonder why I believe I need more money or more friends or less agitation. **Working with goals as a gateway to letting go of suffering in any form is a path to freedom.**

When I set a goal these days, one of the first questions I ask is why? Why do I need that? What will it give me? As an example, a thought arose about setting a goal to be more disciplined about writing. When I asked why, the answer was I wanted to stay tapped into creativity.

We are creative beings by nature. We feel more alive, more tuned in, more connected when engaged in creative activities. The free flow that happens in creative activities echoes the feeling of being in flow with the universe, which is my ultimate goal.

ENTHUSIASM

While this book is definitely not a guide to writing goals, if you set a goal that feels exciting to you, your path will be that much easier. If one friend invited you to come over and help her organize her house and another invited you to go to a concert, which are you more apt to want to do? (And yes, I know some of you do love your organizing…)

It's the same premise when you're asking yourself to do something. **If it's fun, it gets done.**

Rather than "I allow myself to lose 20 pounds," try "I allow myself to enjoy my healthy kick-ass body," or "I allow myself to show off my washboard abs." Engage with whatever evokes the most excitement. Moving toward something that naturally invokes enthusiasm is much easier than trying to accomplish a goal because you think you should or have to.

You may be wondering how letting go can help in achieving goals, especially since we are so often told the exact opposite. We've been instructed to work harder or longer and to invest more time, money and energy. **We are led to believe we don't have what we want because we are not trying hard enough or wanting it enough.** This has significantly increased the reluctance among many individuals to set goals. In my experience, there are many reasons we don't achieve our goals, but laziness is not the key factor.

BLOCKS TO ACHIEVING GOALS

There are three primary areas where we run into trouble with goals.

The first roadblock is setting the wrong goal. And by wrong, I mean only wrong for you. Many people don't know (or won't allow themselves to know) what makes their heart sing. **The goals we set are often based on what society, parents, spouses, or bosses say we should want.** There are two inherent problems with this: 1) if someone else tells us what to do, it automatically sets up resistance, and 2) internal excitement is what drives action; if you are not excited about a goal, you are much less likely to achieve it.

The first important aspect of setting goals is selecting one about which you are personally excited. There's a section in *The New Earth*, by Eckhart Tolle, which talks about the three modalities of awakened doing: acceptance, enjoyment and enthusiasm. In *The New Earth*, he writes that enjoyment will replace wanting as the motivating power behind people's actions. Through enjoyment, you link into the universal creative power. **Add a vision of enjoyment to a goal and the energy field or vibrational frequency changes.** Tolle says, "At the height of creative activity fueled by enthusiasm, there will be enormous intensity and energy behind what you do. You will feel like an arrow that is moving toward the target—and enjoying the journey."[21]

The second roadblock arises from internal conflict. Even if you are excited about a goal, there are likely conflicting beliefs (some conscious, some not) about reaching that goal. For instance, you may want to lose weight and may not want to give up the social aspects of eating. You may want more money in the bank but have been raised to believe rich people are self-absorbed. If you don't acknowledge and release these conflicts, they will be in the way of attaining the goal. Your subconscious beliefs can sabotage your desired achievements.

Emotions are at the center of the third roadblock. Many say you must want something with all your heart to have it. As first covered in Chapter 7 on habits, wanting affirms lack. If you think about anything you really, really want, whether it's money, peace, or a relationship, you can feel in your body that sense of not having or not being enough. When we want or lust for something, we are very literally reminding ourselves of lack or limitation. I'm a firm believer in the maxim, "What you pay attention to multiplies," and when we are wanting, we are paying attention to lack. We definitely are not interested in less of what we desire! As you uncover what's driving your surface desires, you can explore deeper and discover what is most true and authentic for you. It can also be helpful to reframe the question from "What do I want?" to **"What wants to come into form through me?"** This question can take us out of ego-driven desires and help us tap into the energy that moves and creates through us.

Childhood experiences can also sabotage goals. The beliefs you uncovered in any of the previous practices in this book may be holding you back.

116

Bringing movement to our desires and the accompanying beliefs and emotions can reveal places where we are stymied by limitation. We may also find that we don't really want what we thought we wanted.

GOALS PRACTICES

Many practices from earlier chapters overlap with goals. Beliefs (Chapter 4), emotions (Chapter 5), resistance and lack of motivation (Chapter 6), habits of procrastination and worry (Chapter 7) and relationships (Chapter 8) all play a role in both supporting and blocking us from having what we want. Our life experiences are entwined with our desires. Which is why **working with goals can be a powerful path to freedom.**

PRACTICE #73: I WANT

In this practice, we go deeper into the feeling of wanting that we first visited in Chapter 1 and Practice #2. We create goals because we want something. Human nature bends to longing for more, or sometimes less, of something or someone. In this practice, we work with the natural tendency of desire as a means of loosening its grip.

Once you've set your goals or identified what you want, let yourself feel what sensations arise when wanting those particular objects or experiences. Notice if any resistance or aversion arises as you contemplate allowing yourself to want something.

Let yourself want whatever it is as much as you do. If you were to communicate that desire without words, what would it look like? You could pretend to be playing charades. Give yourself permission to go deep into longing and find what movements express wanting. Notice the accompanying thoughts and feelings. Notice fear of not getting what you want, and also any fear of having it. You may find some of both. There may be beliefs, including "That's not allowed" or "It's never going to happen." Remember that you are not your beliefs and that this practice is not about figuring out how to get what you want, but to uncover what might be lurking below the surface of your longing.

When you feel ready, let go of the movement associated with wanting. If you showed wanting as a reach or a grasp, open your hand or drop your arm. If you felt wanting more in your eyes, let them soften. You might have even felt desire in your chest or stomach. If so, let that sensation soften. Again, what are you aware of? Do you feel like you've given up? Or perhaps you feel some relief and lightness. Keep playing with movements associated with wanting and notice what thoughts and feelings surface for you.

PRACTICE #74: I DON'T KNOW

It's common for people not to know what they want. This can be a lifelong habit (often informed by being told as children what we do and don't want) and sometimes not knowing is a temporary or situational experience. Either way, this practice can be helpful.

Find the movements you associate with not knowing. Those could be a shrug of the shoulders, moving without direction or walking in circles. Whatever movement you choose or spontaneously arises, allow it. Be the scarecrow from *The Wizard of Oz* if that resonates.

So often, judgment accompanies not knowing. The mind says, "Well, you should know," but sometimes we just don't. The time may not be right and there may be critical information we don't have yet. For now, could you allow *not knowing* to have some room to move in and through you? Becoming comfortable with what is present is the first step to inviting change. You might find that embracing *not knowing* leads you to being able to find knowing.

PRACTICE #75: FIND KNOWING

When you start to pay attention, you'll find many opportunities in your daily life where you do know. Everyday activities such as deciding what to wear, what to eat and how to respond to people and situations give us opportunities to find answers. Start by noticing all you do know and all the ways you experience knowing. When dressing, do you imagine how you would feel in the red shirt versus the purple shirt? When ordering dinner, do you stop and sense how fried rice versus salad might affect your body? Do you pause before responding to questions or are you more often automatic? When you identify the methods you are already comfortable using daily, you can transition to using the same methodologies with what feels like a more complex issue. If you've been debating about going back to school, feel into that experience in your body. Is it allowed? Is it a strong yes, a soft maybe, or a resounding no? Thinking about a big career, moving to a new town, starting a new relationship or a new adventure? Imagine doing whatever you are considering doing and see how it feels internally. Imagine you do know the answer and see what that evokes in you. Often, below the thoughts and feelings about what's allowed, we find knowing.

PRACTICE #76: SO MANY OPTIONS

Often, we are stuck in believing there is only one correct path, when in truth, there are multiple ways to achieve almost any goal.

Begin by walking directly across the room toward something you've chosen to represent the object of your desire, and then experiment with zigzagging, walking backward or sideways, crawling, jumping, or spinning to get there. Feeling different options in your body may wake your mind up to possibilities you hadn't previously considered in achieving your goals.

PRACTICE #77: FEEL IT DONE

Imagine your goal achieved or desire fulfilled. What would change in your life? How would your body feel or move once you have attained the goal and its results? Is there excitement and enthusiasm? What does excitement and enthusiasm feel like in your body and how could it express itself? It might help to remember your young self on Christmas morning or Chanukkah or on your birthday or a vacation. That little one can help you remember the movements that conveyed your excitement. Allowing yourself to move with enthusiasm and joy will support motivation and action.

If you experience heaviness or overwhelm or aversion, that's also valuable information. You might want to reconsider or modify your goal.

PRACTICE #78: RECEIVING

To give and receive are one in truth.

—A Course in Miracles, Lesson 108[1]

When setting goals, the energy is often fixed on advancing somewhere or acquiring something. Yet, many people are not comfortable with receiving and accepting. Whether receiving compliments, physical or emotional support, or material items, these offerings are often met with discomfort or rejection. If you are not able to receive, your goals could show up only to find a shuttered door and no access.

Begin this practice by noticing what you already allow in each day. Pay attention to how you receive air in every breath, how you allow the soothing effect of water in the shower, how you exchange affection with your children or four-legged friends. Start paying more attention to the experience of receiving in your body. In this practice, we see how softening and opening can assist not only in letting go, but also in letting in.

Expand your practice wherever you can. If you're in the habit of pushing away compliments, next time you receive a compliment, deeply breathe and take in the praise as best you can. If you say no to others' offers of help, look for where you could say, "Yes, thank you." It won't always be a "Yes," and that's as it should be for many reasons. Sometimes others have an idea of what might be helpful that doesn't line up with what we need, and in those cases, by all means, say, "No, and thank you."

Learning to receive is also a gift to others. If you're someone who loves to give, notice how much you enjoy the other's ability to graciously receive and mimic that grace in your own acceptance. **These reciprocal energies need each other.**

PRACTICE #79: GIVING

Sometimes, goals ask us to give up or contribute more than we want to or more than we're comfortable with. Whether the ask is time, financial investment, free products or materials, we may have some internal resistance to this giving. Or our giving may come with expectations that get in the way of the natural energy flow. **When giving is accompanied by wanting in return, it becomes a transactional contract.** There's nothing wrong with contracts, as long as both parties are consciously entering them. Practicing giving selflessly can connect you with your true nature, which naturally gives without wanting.

To practice giving without expectation, again think about ways you are already doing that. Children and animals are often the recipients of unconditional giving. If you have one or more of these (children or animals), reflect for a moment on what you're happy to give them. They may give nothing in exchange. If you've been waiting for acknowledgment and gratitude, turn your attention to the fact that you are able to give, and enjoy that.

Where you can, expand your practice. Offer a compliment to a stranger, share your office snacks with a co-worker. You might even decide to go out and buy a great big bag of jellybeans so you can walk around and spread some cheer for no reason other than to give.

PRACTICE #80: TAP INTO INSPIRATION

Sometimes the inspiration required to achieve your goal, or some aspect of your goal, may be absent when needed. Often, in this scenario, walking away and coming back when the inspiration is there works. But sometimes, there's a deadline that won't wait. How do you tap into the spirit of the project or task?

This practice is quite literal—tap into inspiration.

Tapping energy points on the body signals your nervous system to reduce fear, anger, stress and grief, and activates areas of the brain that help with problem-solving and managing emotions.[22]

You could do lots of research on this practice and find specific tapping techniques for inspiration. Or you could just start tapping on various spots on your face, your head, your hands and see what happens. See if your stomach wants some taps or the back of your thighs need waking up. As you tap, keep in mind the words "tapping into" and pay attention. Are you tapping something into yourself? Are you tapping into something beyond yourself? Tap your feet or your pen and find some rhythm! And then maybe that rhythm turns into the rhythm of your fingers on the keyboard or the rhythm of painting your kitchen. You may have found the rhythm of inspiration!

PRACTICE #81: GIVE UP

Do those words create a reaction in you? If so, you aren't alone. We have been brainwashed to think giving up is quitting and quitting is bad. You may push yourself into doing something you've decided is not for you, so as not to be a quitter. You may have stayed in an unhealthy relationship because leaving is giving up. These beliefs are well worth challenging. Sometimes, giving up is exactly the medicine we need. We can give up for an hour, a day, or forever. You may even want to give up being a parent, or a therapist, or whatever it is that occupies most of your time. Do it for an hour, more if you can. Even taking short breaks can reignite enthusiasm.

We could also see giving up more literally. What if you saw giving up as giving over and up to a higher intelligence? That's certainly a distinct perspective.

Let yourself find the traditional movements associated with giving up in the body—head drooping, arms hanging, maybe falling to the floor. Play with and exaggerate the movements of dropping everything, literally letting go. Feel the pressure release and the relaxation that can happen when giving up.

Then feel giving up in the literal sense. **Give up to the angels, your ancestors, your higher self, to the birds, to the universe.** Everything is there for the taking. You might add some words: "Here, take this. I've been carrying it too long. I don't know what to do with it," or "Thank you for taking this. I could really use some help." Whatever wants to come out of your mouth is allowed. And you can back up your words with physical movements like turning your palms up and raising your arms and imagining you are presenting an offering. Or you could write down what you want to give up and then light a match or a candle to it and let it go up in smoke (taking all necessary precautions and safety measures, of course).

CHAPTER 10
THE EVERYDAY HABIT OF LETTING GO

I've provided an encyclopedia of ways to use your body and movement to support letting go and living with more ease and flow. The exercises are designed to help you rely less on thinking and more on the wisdom of your body and intuition.

Much like exercise or meditation, letting go needs to be an ongoing practice to maintain wellbeing. While it is possible for upsets based on past events to completely resolve through letting go practices, the world is quick to offer more opportunities to lose our peace on a regular basis.

THE POWER OF LETTING GO IN THE MOMENT

Learning to catch the old go-to responses of agitation, judgment and upset becomes easier the more we practice. And the more we practice, the more likely we are to develop a new go-to response of letting go. **Or better yet, not picking up the upset or taking on the agitation in the first place.**

My therapy clients have been known to ask, "How long do I have to keep doing this?" And, by "this," they don't mean therapy. They are asking about the process of paying attention to their feelings and the need to process new experiences. I lovingly laugh when I say "Forever."

There was a time when I also felt impatient to end my practices, and a time when I thought I had moved past the need to practice (I hear my guides and friends on the other side laughing). That was over thirty years ago. I have since learned to embrace the work of introspection and self-discovery and hope I will continue to all my days.

Creating an ongoing practice could be challenging for you. Or you may find, it just happens. You may get out of your car after being stuck in traffic and start intentionally shaking. You may watch the news and instead of sitting and complaining, you'll stand up and stomp your feet. Or maybe you'll be sitting in a business meeting and become aware of your throat tightening as you muster to speak. The more you make body awareness and letting go a daily practice, the more it happens spontaneously.

If you're struggling, remind yourself it takes time to develop a new habit (studies say 18 to 254 days, with 66 days being the average).[23] Finding your personal motivation will also help. Once you begin developing a regular practice of letting go, you'll start to notice you're not stuck with the same old thought, the ongoing worry or resentment for days on end. And you may even become a little addicted to your daily movement practices of letting go.

LIST OF SOME EVERYDAY PRACTICES

I recommend committing to the same practice every day at the same time, or committing to 5 minutes of conscious movement a day. Decide to embed certain practices into your workday, such as setting a reminder to go off hourly, or at a specific time once or twice or even three times a day, reminding you to walk around your desk and check in with your body, or get up and shake for 30 seconds.

Here's a very partial list of practices you can keep in your awareness (or on your wall!):

1. Check in with one body part a day
2. Pause throughout the day to check in with sensations
3. Notice all the things you're naturally letting go of moment to moment (including breath)
4. At the end of the day, see if there is anything since morning that you're holding on to—what would it take to let it go?
5. Open this book to any practice and do it
6. Pay more attention to breath
7. Notice tightness and contraction and allow yourself to soften and open
8. Go outside and interact with nature (feel the sun on your face, the ground beneath your feet, the wind on your skin) and allow your senses to be awakened

Sometimes, it's helpful to couple a new habit with an existing behavior. If you often spend time waiting in line or picking up a child from school, use that time to roll your head or your shoulders. When you walk the dog, check your pace—are you walking at a speed that feels comfortable for you? (The dog can adjust.) Or could you growl with the dogs or purr/whine with the cats or tweet with the birds?

There are so many more practices I'm aware of than I included in this book, which means there are millions more I'm not aware of. Feel free and empowered to develop your own practices to support what you need in any given moment. Don't attach to any one practice; instead, pay attention to how your needs change day to day and develop new practices when inspired.

NOTES

1. Foundation for Inner Peace, A Course in Miracles (Foundation for Inner Peace, 1976).

2. Michael A. Singer, *Living Untethered: Beyond the Human Predicament* (New Harbinger Publications / Noetic Books, 2021).

3. Michael Newton, Michael Newton Institute, accessed 2025, https://www.newtoninstitute.org.

4. Lester Levenson, Sedona Training Associates, https://www.sedona.com/Lester-Levenson.

5. Kerry Ward, "Beginner's Guide to Palm Reading," *Cosmopolitan*, November 12, 2019.

6. Melanie Smithson, "Reclaiming an Adult Relationship to Play" (Smithson Clinic, Inc., 1998), https://www.smithsonclinic.com/product-page/reclaiming-an-adult-relationship-toplay.

7. "Let There Be Peace on Earth" by Jill-Jackson Miller and Sy Miller, written 1955.

8. Gabrielle Roth, *Maps to Ecstasy: Teachings of an Urban Shaman* (Nataraj Pub., 1989).

9. Susan Aposhyan, *Natural Intelligence: Body-Mind Integration and Human Development* (Lippincott Williams & Wilkins, 1999).

10. "Love Shack," by the B-52's, track 4 on *Cosmic Thing*, Reprise Records, 1989.

11. Eckhart Tolle, *The Power of Now: A Guide to Spiritual Enlightenment* (Namaste Publishing, 1999).

12. Candace Pert, *Molecules of Emotion: The Science Behind Mind-Body Medicine* (Simon & Schuster, 1999).

13. Walter Hagen, *The Walter Hagen Story* (Simon & Schuster, 1956).

14. Jonathan Safran Foer, *Extremely Loud and Incredibly Close* (Houghton Mifflin, 2005), 180.

15. Dan Millman, *Way of the Peaceful Warrior: A Book That Changes Lives* (Jeremy P. Tarcher, 1980).

16. "Mikey Likes It," Life Cereal ad by Quaker Oats Company (ad agency Foote, Cone & Belding), first aired on television 1972.

17. "On Feeling Resistance," Project Self, accessed April 2025, www.projectself.co.uk/guides/lost/resistance/on-feeling-resistance.

18. Julie Andrews, vocalist, "A Spoonful of Sugar," composed by Robert B. Sherman and Richard M. Sherman, track 5 on *Mary Poppins: Original Cast Soundtrack*, Buena Vista Records, 1964.

19. Gruder, D. Ethical Personal Power Effectiveness Training Manual. 2017, Integrity Revolution Press, USA.

20. Albert Mehrabian, *Silent Messages: Implicit Communication of Emotions and Attitudes* (Wadsworth, 1971).

21. Eckhart Tolle, *A New Earth: Awakening to Your Life's Purpose* (Dutton / Penguin Group, 2005).

22. Donna Eden and David Feinstein, *Tapping: Self-Healing with the Transformative Power of Energy Psychology* (Sounds True, 2024).

23. Phillippa Lally et al., "How Are Habits Formed: Modelling Habit Formation in the Real World," *European Journal of Social Psychology* 40, no. 6 (2010): 998–1009.

BOOKS

Caldwell, Christine. *Getting Our Bodies Back: Recovery, Healing, and Transformation Through Body-Centered Psychotherapy.* Shambhala Publications, 1996.

Caldwell, Christine. *Bodyfulness: Somatic Practices for Presence, Empowerment, and Waking Up in This Life.* Shambala Publications, 2018.

Donaldson, Fred. *Playing by Heart: The Vision and Practice of Belonging.* Health Communications, Inc., 1993.

Dwoskin, Hale. *The Sedona Method: Your Key to Lasting Happiness, Success, Peace and Emotional Well-Being.* Sedona Press, 2003.

Keleman, Stanley. *Your Body Speaks Its Mind.* Center Press, 1975.

Levy, Fran. *Dance Movement Therapy: A Healing Art.* American Alliance for Health, Physical Education, Recreation, and Dance, 1988.

Lowen, Alexander. *The Spirituality of the Body: Bioenergetics for Grace and Harmony.* MacMillan Publishing Co., 1990.

McGonigal, Kelly. *The Willpower Instinct: How Self-Control Works, Why It Matters, and What You Can Do to Get More of It.* Penguin Group, 2012.

McGonigal, Kelly. *The Joy of Movement: How Exercise Helps Us Find Happiness, Hope, Connection, and Courage.* Avery, 2019

Nachmanovitch, Stephen. *Free Play: The Power of Improvisation in Life and the Arts.* G.P. Putnam's Sons, 1990.

Roth, Gabrielle. *Maps to Ecstasy: The Healing Power of Movement.* Nataraj Publishing, 1998.

Singer, Michael A. *The Untethered Soul: The Journey Beyond Yourself.* New Harbinger Publications, 2007.

Singer, Michael A. *Living Untethered: Beyond the Human Predicament.* New Harbinger Publications, 2022.

TRAININGS, SEMINARS AND AUDIO PROGRAMS

5Rhythms®, Gabrielle Roth, http://www.5rhythms.com/

MA Program in Somatic Counseling Psychology, Naropa University, Boulder, Colorado, https://www.naropa.edu/programs/graduate-academics/clinical-mental-healthcounseling/somatic-counseling/

Moving with Life, Zuza Engler, https://zuzaengler.com/

Soul Motion International, https://soulmotioninternational.com/

The 5Rhythm® and Somatic Arts—Reviving Embodied Intelligence, Chloe Goodwin, Santa Fe, New Mexico, http://chloegoodwin.com/

The Sedona Method, audio recordings, books, retreats and trainings, http://www.sedona.com

ACKNOWLEDGEMENTS

I am a strong advocate of approaching life with a sense of humor and a light-hearted attitude. That said, writing and publishing a book is no joke. And definitely not a one-person job. Many hands went into bringing this book to form, and the wisdom of many teachers is incorporated into its pages.

Hands-on support came from my editors, Sheila Burns and Kimberly Kurzawa. The attention to detail they both provided made me a little crazy, and I am deeply grateful. The cover design process was made fun and easy by Francis at 100 Covers. Amanda Maria, with Land of Photography, was a joy to work with. Alexa Bigwarfe, of Write, Publish, Sell, has provided invaluable resources for every step of the way. The Women in Publishing community is formidable.

Early feedback and support from Deanell Sandoval, Chloe Goodwin, Virginia Swem and Tiffany Grunert was invaluable. I am fortunate to have such smart and kind women in my life.

Words from so many of my teachers found their way directly and indirectly into this book. Sometimes, their words have entwined with my thoughts, and I no longer know their origin. I have been profoundly influenced and changed by Judy Borich, Barbara Flood, Christine Caldwell and Hale Dwoskin.

I am beyond grateful for the gift of dance and movement. I wish I had known sooner what a profound gift my mother was giving me in sharing her love of dance with me. I hope she can feel my gratitude wherever she may be. Gene Acquirre, John Medeiros, Jessica Morningstar Wolf, Randy Miller, Zuza Engler and Chloe Goodwin—you are my heroes. I hope you can feel your presence and influence in my words.

Tracy Gregory allowed me to communicate directly with those on the other side supporting this book. My appreciation for Tracy and the unseen ones knows no bounds.

And finally, my life would not work without the love and support of my husband, Gail Smithson.

ABOUT THE AUTHOR

Melanie Smithson, a dancer since the age of four, is also a Licensed Somatic Psychotherapist, Business Owner, Certified Spiritual Integration Hypnotherapist, and the award-winning author of *Stress Free in 30 Seconds—A Slightly Irreverent Approach to Navigating Life's Challenges*. Through the highs and lows of life, movement has been there to support her in processing, transforming and releasing upsets. For thirty years, she has been sharing the wisdom of the body and the power of movement with her therapy clients and group participants. She is dedicated to broadening access to somatic practices to alleviate suffering, live light-heartedly, and foster a deeper connection to one's inner nature.

She is co-owner of Smithson Clinic, Inc. with her husband, Gail, in Santa Fe, New Mexico, where they live with and serve the ultimate playmate and 100 lb. lapdog, Kyra.

Melanie offers many workshops and trainings (mostly online) for therapists, coaches and others seeking or supporting personal transformation through the body. To learn more, visit http://www.smithsonclinic.com.

MORE WAYS TO MOVE WITH MELANIE

The author, Melanie Smithson, is available for speaking and training events. But don't expect to just sit there and listen. She'll have you up and shaking, bouncing and jiggling, so you can experience the power of movement firsthand. She offers many online groups and is available for individual consultations as well.

For more information:

Visit http://www.smithsonclinic.com,
Email melanie@smithsonclinic.com,
Call/text 303-762-8994.

A GIFT FOR YOU

ALL 81 PRACTICES IN ONE DOCUMENT! AND 10 BONUS PRACTICES!

Need easy access to all the practices? Go to http://smithsonclinic.com/81practices for your downloadable PDF and print your copy for the wall, desk or to carry with you—just the practices for easy reference. You never know when you'll have a movement practice emergency.

You'll find 10 additional practices not in the book, including practices for your relationships with money, success, and parenting.